PRAISE FOR GENESIS

If you think you know the book of Genesis, think again! In her book, *Genesis: Small Stories of a Big God*, Georgia Tanner's extraordinary ability as a story teller merges with her refreshing personal transparency, her God given insights into the lives we all live and a wonderfully deep understanding of the real story of the Bible. The result for you will be what it was for me. 'I see this story in a way I have never seen it before. I see my heart more honestly than I have ever seen it before. And I see Jesus on every page.' This book will move you and mark you - whether you are investigating Jesus for the first time or have followed Him for years. I cannot recommend it with anything but superlatives. You will LOVE this book!

—REV BOB CARGO
Director of Church Planting, Perimeter Church; former Senior Pastor of Intown Community Church

In *Genesis: Small Stories of a Big God*, Georgia Tanner takes our hand and leads us to a safe, comfortable place, far from the shouting match about the nature of the text. In that silence she helps us listen to the stories in a new way. They are no longer ammunition to be fired at our theological enemies. They have become sources of fascination, at once both comforting and immense, good for our weary 21st century souls. Georgia Tanner has given us a wonderful gift.

—JOHN HAMBRICK
Director of Starting Point and Staff Development, Buckhead Church, and author of *Move Toward the Mess*.

I have walked with Georgia in life and personal ministry for years. I'm honored to endorse this beautiful book that will lead you to discover more of God.

—ALLISON HOLLEY
Married Groups Director, North Point Ministries/Buckhead Church

Genesis

In the beginning
was the Word...
John 1:1

Georgia Tanner
12·03·21

Genesis

SMALL STORIES OF A **BIG GOD**

GEORGIA TANNER

Carpenter's Son Publishing

GENESIS
Small Stories of a Big God

Author's Note
We are incredibly fortunate that we have access to so many different versions of the Bible, God's Holy Word! I have primarily used my well-worn *New International Version Study Bible* as I have studied, but I love reading from other versions, and often these translations use a word or a phrase that speaks to me in a meaningful way. God's Word has slowly found its way into my mind and heart, so sometimes my own version is my favorite, which I have noted as *my paraphrase* within the book. I've also italicized some words within verses for emphasis as well as adding my comments in brackets. I gratefully acknowledge that Scripture quoted from the Holy Bible comes from the following translations:

Published by Carpenter's Son Publishing, Franklin, Tennessee

Printed in the United States of America

ISBN: 978-1-949572-02-5

This book is dedicated to Community Bible Study.

As my sister Kathy would affirm, God is good.

To God be the glory!

CONTENTS

THE FAMILY OF GENESIS

God: Creator, Lord, Father, God of Promises, Shield, Great Reward, El Shaddai, Almighty One, God Most High, Shepherd, Rock of Israel.

Adam and Eve: Man and woman, created in God's image. They make a really bad decision that shuts down the Garden of Eden.

The Serpent: Satan, the devil, liar, enemy of God and God's family. Likes to talk.

Cain: Adam and Eve's first son. Introduces murder and lies and is banished from his people.

Abel: Second son. Pleases God, killed by brother.

Seth: Third son. We follow his long life to Noah.

Enoch: Seth's descendant who never dies.

Noah: Seth's descendant who obeys God and builds an ark before the rains come.

Shem: Noah's son. Father of the Semites. One of his descendants is the Hebrew, Abraham. Settles in the Ancient Near East, Asia.

Japheth: Noah's son. Father of the Gentiles. Descendants are European, Caucasian.

Ham: Noah's son. Father of the Arab nations. Descendants include Canaanites, Egyptians, and some Africans.

Abram: Friend of God, Father Abraham, husband of Sarai, father of Ishmael and Isaac. Prepares to sacrifice his son Isaac at God's request.

Sarai: Wife (and half sister!) of Abram. Is renamed Sarah. Mother of Isaac. Has an unusual solution to being childless. Her grave becomes the first land Abraham will own.

Hagar: Handmaiden of Sarai. Is offered to Abram by Sarai. Mother of Ishmael. Spends a lot of time in the desert.

Lot: Nephew of Abram. Chooses city life in Sodom. Is rescued by angels. Wife turns into pillar of salt. Unwittingly fathers children by his own daughters who become the Moabites and the Ammonites.

Melchizedek: King of Salem, priest of the Most High God. Blesses Abram. Prototype of Messiah.

David: Future descendant of Abraham. Shepherd. Psalmist. King of Israel.

Jesus: Future descendant of Abraham and David, Messiah (God's Anointed One), King, Priest, Living Water, Good Shepherd, Sacrificial Lamb, Stairway to Heaven.

Ishmael: Son of Abraham by handmaiden Hagar. Marries the wrong sort of women, has twelve sons, and lives in conflict with those around him.

Isaac: Son of Abraham by wife Sarah. Father lays him on an altar. Marries Rebekah and has twins: Jacob and Esau. Loves Esau most.

The Servant: Abraham trusts him to find a good wife for Isaac from among his folks back home, where he finds Rebekah.

Rebekah: Strong spirited. Wife of Isaac, mother of twins: Jacob and Esau. Loves Jacob most and encourages him to deceive Daddy Isaac.

Keturah: "Footnote wife" of Abraham after Sarah dies. Keturah bears him children, but no interest here.

Esau: Firstborn twin son of Isaac and Rebekah. Sells his birthright to his brother Jacob. Hairy hunter. Alias: Edom.

Jacob: Second-born twin son of Isaac and Rebekah. Always struggles with man and God. Steals Esau's blessing. Dreams of stairway to heaven. Stressful family life. Is renamed "Israel." Twelve sons become twelve tribes of Israel.

Laban: Brother of Rebekah, father of Rachel and Leah, father-in-law of Jacob. Tricky.

Rachel: Younger daughter of Laban, beloved wife of Jacob, mother of sons Joseph and Benjamin.

Leah: Older cross-eyed daughter of Laban. Jacob is tricked into marrying her. Mother of sons Reuben, Simeon, Levi, Judah, Issachar, Zebulun, and daughter Dinah.

Zilpah: Leah's handmaid who bears two sons for Jacob: Gad and Asher.

Bilhah: Rachel's handmaid who bears two sons for Jacob: Dan and Naphtali.

Shechem: Canaanite son of Hamor the Hittite. Falls in love with Dinah and eventually invites everyone in town to a little circumcision party to get in good with her brothers. Is murdered by Jacob's sons Simeon and Levi.

Reuben: Jacob's firstborn son who has sex with Jacob's concubine Bilhah.

Joseph: Jacob's favorite son, to whom he gives a colorful coat. Dreamer. Is sold into slavery by brothers, then rescued by God to save Egypt and his entire family.

Judah: Jacob's fourth-born son. Canaanite culture. Unknowingly has sex with daughter-in-law. Eventually takes responsibility for his actions.

Tamar: Canaanite woman. Is widowed twice while married to Judah's sons, but takes control of her future by disguising herself as a temple prostitute and getting pregnant by her father-in-law Judah.

Benjamin: Youngest son of Jacob and Rachel. Joseph uses Benjamin to test the integrity of his older brothers.

PREFACE

I wanted to read and understand God's Word, but I could not figure out where to begin. Then one day, a dear friend invited me to a nondenominational Bible study. I didn't know if I would make it through the year, but within two years I trained to lead an evening class of Community Bible Study as Teaching Director. Eighteen years later I am humbled by the incredible teaching I have received and the inspiring women, men, teens, and children I have shared this journey with. God has pulled me out of my darkness and confusion and has drawn me into His glorious light, where wisdom is freely given.

I am neither a scholar nor an intellectual trained in religious studies. Kind reader, take warning: These are the words of a woman who is madly in love with the God whose voice is in my ear as I read His Word. My prayer is that hearing His voice will bring you great comfort and joy.

SMALL STORIES
This Is Where We Begin

As a little girl, I grew up listening to great storytelling. In the winter we all sat on the back porch at my grandparents' house on Sunday afternoons. After World War II my dad and his brother enclosed what had been a screened porch, and it became the winter gathering spot. The long line of windows across the back wall let in the afternoon light and gave you a good view of the train tracks behind the house. A gray Formica kitchen table stood in the center of the room, with matching chairs held together by duct tape. The cozy space also had a refrigerator and a threadbare rug covering the concrete floor. For additional seating, we had an ancient sofa and a metal glider covered with so many old quilts that I never realized it was outdoor furniture.

On one side of the center of that room stood the most important seat in the house: the wooden rocking chair where Grandpa sat. It sported an ancient coat of cracked green paint, and you could easily see smooth finger outlines showing down to the warmth of the wood where his hands had gently rubbed the paint away over the years.

All conversation in that room, then, centered around Grandpa. Gentle and soft-spoken, he was the patriarch of a very Southern family. Great stories were told and heard in that room. The stories often had to be paused in the middle of telling—to wait for the laughter to die down. All the Tanner adults were great storytellers, and I never wanted to miss a single word—even though I had probably heard the story before.

Those stories gave me a strong sense of belonging. I felt safe. Surrounded by love and security. My grandparents and aunts and uncles told stories of places I didn't know and people who had come before me. There was history there. And continuity. What had come before felt solid and sure and real to me, and I knew it would continue forward as it had for generations.

Later, when I met my husband's family, it was as if I had walked into that old back porch of my grandparents' house. His large family of aunts and uncles and cousins told their own stories and laughed and put their arms around you as if you were their own. They, too, were storytellers. Their stories told of who they were. Their stories told of their past and offered a promise of who they would be in the future. Their stories connected them, wrapping them in an unseen fabric of love and security.

In His unfathomable wisdom, God Himself chose to connect with us—His creation, His children—by telling us His stories. When I read His stories, I have to stop and let them sink in. I want to be there in the place and time when these stories were first told. I want to hear the voice of the storyteller. I want to look into the faces of the listeners. I want to hear the laughter—or feel the brokenness that the story was meant to ease. I want to understand the wisdom buried there.

For me now, every story starts with God—the first Story-teller. I belong to God's family, gathered with others, sitting on His back porch, listening to His words, looking into His face, hearing His laughter, soaking up His truth and His love. God is so big that we cannot begin to comprehend Him, and so He tells us about Himself through "small stories." This is where we start: with His words, with His stories. *Small Stories of a Big God.*

This is really not morning devotional reading. It is more like end-of-the-day, ready-for-bed, lamplight reading. So pull out your Bible and start with the Scripture passage I have listed for each chapter. If you can read it out loud—the way it was originally intended—you will find God's words to you are incredibly powerful. Then you can read my musings on God's story. Throughout these stories, I write the conversations I hear between the lines. I write what I think they certainly must have been thinking. In every story I see everyday people struggling with how small and broken they are. My hope, and my prayer, is that these small stories will help you see the compassionate heart and hear the amazing truths of a very big God!

1
ONCE UPON A TIME
Read Genesis 1–2:3

66 **I**n the beginning ..." Genesis 1:1 reads like the stuff of fairy tales. Can you hear it? Sit quietly and listen: the voice of God telling Adam and Eve the story. Sitting by a campfire in the cool of the evening, embers glowing, the animals Adam had named looking on while settling down for the night. The lion and the lamb curled up together. God's voice, quiet and steady, telling their favorite bedtime story: how it all began.

If I were the one telling the story, I would have spent more time telling about designing the patterns on the lizards or choosing the colors for the birds' feathers. I would have gotten carried away explaining the millions and millions of insects, from hard-shelled and creeping to wispy and winged. But no, God tells the story differently. God spent days on light and water. Finally on day three came land and its plants and trees with their own life-producing seeds. Interesting, this touch—that He chose to allow living things to produce more of their own. The Creator allowed His creation to create.

Then He paused to put lights in the sky. Again, with my little human brain, if I was making all this up, it seems like the sun and moon would have come earlier, with the creation of light on day one or the creation of the heavens on day two. But no, God had a very specific order. He wanted us to understand order, so he gave us the concept of time on this fourth day. He gave us time that would be marked off by the stars and the sun and the moon: time specific to us here on earth. Time that we could keep by way of "seasons and days and years" (v. 14).

Now just ponder for a moment if God had not given us the marking of time. How would you know it's Sunday and dinner will be at Grandma's? How would we know it's the first day of school for Ellie or that the latest movie we want to see starts at 7:45 on Friday night? How would we know we've been married almost thirty-two years or that it's time to feed the dog? Time was an interesting concept for God to create. I don't know that I would have thought of it had it never existed. Declared good, the fourth day came to a close.

Then came the fifth day, just for creating the living things in the seas and the sky. We still haven't seen all that is there in the heights of the heavens or in the depths of the seas. Then we rush headlong into that deadline of the sixth day with all the creatures that inhabit dry ground: livestock, wild animals, and creatures that crawl. It seems like a lot to bite off in one day, and He hadn't even gotten to the really good part—us!

Suddenly the conversation changed. He had been speaking everything into existence—"Let there be ... Let there be ..." But then on this sixth day, He seemed to be working with someone else. Listen: "Then God said, 'Let *us* make man in *our* image, in *our* likeness'" (v. 26, my emphasis). Whoa! Stop! Did you hear that? God just became *plural*. I think there was someone else in the room sharing this creative process with Him!

From my understanding, in the original Hebrew, the word here for *God* is plural but used as a singular. Then the "us" and "our" is plural, which sort of contradicts the idea of a singular God. God is more complex and deeper than anything else that exists, than anything He has created. (Which actually makes sense, right?) Somehow, our God is one God in three persons. He will reveal himself as a united Trinity, three in one; Father, Holy Spirit, Son.[1]

For now, here in the beginning, in verse 2 we are introduced to the "Spirit of God," and before we have gotten through this first chapter, we are being made in the "image" of God—something that has tangible, identifiable, maybe physical properties. Profoundly, we are told that we (both male and female) have been created to look like or reflect His image (v. 27). God is spirit. And God has an image that can be reflected in us. This is wonderful to think about.

But we are not done yet, because, in addition to being created in His image, we have been given responsibility: to care for everything—to care for every other living thing on our earth. His exact words were "rule over" (v. 26). If we have been created in His image, then that tells us what He does: He rules over. Suddenly in one sentence, we are introduced to ideas of responsibility, provision, stewardship, justice, and purpose. We, the creation, are like the Creator. The words we speak are to be for good. The work of our hands is to be for good.

We start to see clearly the face of God—the One who created something "good" out of the vastness of nothingness. It seems to be important to Him—to create something valuable and worthy. His creation reflected the character, the values of the Creator. "God saw all that he had made, and it was *very good*" (v. 31, my emphasis). In looking at His creation, I think we can say the same thing of the Creator.

Right behind that comes an interesting little note about our diet: we were all vegetarians in the beginning. Did you see that in verse 29? "Then God said, 'I give you every seed-bearing plant on the face of the whole earth and every tree that has fruit with seed in it. They will be yours for food.'" Not only us humans, but also "everything that has the breath of life in it" was given "every green plant for food" (v. 30). The eagles weren't snatching baby squirrels from their nests to feed their young. The mountain lions weren't sitting on the rock cliffs waiting for some hapless cowboy to come riding by. It was not until after the great flood and the newly formed rainbow that meat showed up on our menu. I guess that made things simpler for a while.

But we still aren't done, because we have only ended day six—and I am sure you have noticed our world marks off time in periods of seven days. This seventh day was so very important to God that He declared it "holy" (2:3).

What does a holy day look like? There is an incredibly lovely scene in *The Fiddler on the Roof* movie when the family gathers around the dinner table for Shabbat dinner, beginning with Sabbath prayer. I once had the honor of spending a Friday evening with my nephew's family friends, who are Orthodox Jews, as they celebrated their Shabbat meal. In many ways, it was like that beautiful scene in the movie. We gathered around a large table at sunset, every seat filled with family and friends. Candles were lit, hands washed, prayer offered with a ceremonial glass of wine, and during dinner, they discussed the Scriptures and the week's teachings, and they sang songs in Hebrew. It was magical. It was one of the most fascinating dinners I have ever enjoyed—and it challenges me to follow that example. Slow down. Enjoy the people and the gifts God has given us. Rest today and remember that this day is holy.

God's seventh day was a gift—to Himself and to us. "Rest. Enjoy what I have created. Enjoy all that is good." God gave us the one thing we constantly say we don't have enough of: time to enjoy the wonders of life. "Here," God the Creator says, "I am setting a whole day aside—twenty-four hours—for you to rest. For you to breathe deep. For you to renew. For you to look at Me." It is enough. It is good.

This is our first glimpse of God and His story of the beginning. This was the universe before science and philosophy and religion. This is a life we still love to imagine. God created a universe with a world with a garden with creatures in the sky, the land, the sea. Everything within it was in perfect harmony. There was no guilt, no shame, no killing, no hurt or pain.

Breathe deep. This is the world of God. Can you hear the birds singing? It is the last few moments of daylight and a breeze is in the air.

2
INTRODUCING GOD AND HIS GOODNESS
Read Genesis 2:4–25

I love to tell my children the stories of when they were born. Those first moments spoke volumes about who they were as they entered this world. It was the age of natural childbirth and the beginning of birthing suites. My son was born with the help of a hot bath to ease the pain and a kind midwife who sat at the end of my hospital bed, matter-of-factly encouraging me when I decided I could not do this. "You are the only one who can," she told me. And I did. My son was born wide-eyed and alert, with not a single cry. They placed him in my arms and he looked straight into my eyes, curious and peaceful.

My daughter was a different story. My calmness during labor convinced the midwife on call that I was not ready for the hospital, so she sent me to the doctor's office instead. You see it coming, don't you? They, too, took their time getting me into the room, doing all the doctor's office check-in procedures, taking my temperature, and weighing me before finally hooking me up to the monitor that registered my nice strong, steady contractions. Within moments of the midwife entering the room, everything changed. Her urgency sent an electric charge through the air. The baby was crowning. They ran for the pediatrician, who was down the hall (six months pregnant herself!), they called an ambulance, and two pushes later there was a baby girl in my midwife's arms. There was silence. I opened my eyes to see the midwife's worried face. Finally, there was the shrill cry of my girl as she took her first breath. And relieved laughter from the midwife before she said, "Ah ... we've got a breath holder!"

It is the telling sign of life: breathing. I love reading the story of Adam's first breath. Michelangelo's *Creation of Adam* in the Sistine Chapel is a powerful portrayal of that life-giving moment of God leaning forward, the moment before His finger touches Adam's. But the story told here in Genesis is mind-blowing: "The Lord God formed the man from the dust of the ground and breathed into his nostrils the breath of life, and the man became a living being" (2:7). Think of the intimacy of God, bending down to place His lips to Adam's, to breathe His life-giving breath into the lifeless form of Adam. It is so personal. It is so intimate. It is something we take for granted, breathing in and breathing out—right now—the breath of God.

Suddenly we know something very amazing about this Creator God: He touches us. He formed us; He breathes His life-giving breath into us. It is a loving connection that establishes our very being. In this retelling of the creation account, His name changes to "the Lord God." He has lordship over His creation ... and over us.

It is time to stop looking so hard at the creation and take a good look at this Creator, the Lord God, teller of the story. From looking at the "good" He created, we have already decided that creation reflects the goodness of His character. What else do we see in this newly created world that tells us more about this Lord God?

He provided a garden as a home for Adam. There were no rainy days, for God watered the garden from underground streams. A river flowed in the garden that separated into four mighty rivers, two of which are lost to us now. Trees, beautiful and fruit-bearing, grew in the garden and were good to eat. There was gold, aromatic resin, and beautiful black onyx: resources pleasing to the senses. God created a world that would bring pleasure to His creation. God had created the perfect permanent vacation.

In addition to all of this, God gave Adam purpose: He entrusted him with care of the earth, introducing the ideas of responsibility and ownership. We also see our creative God sharing the creative process by entrusting Adam with the privilege of naming the animals! In the naming, God gave Adam something else: the desire for relationship. God gave man a longing for companionship with someone who was made like him.

Man and woman. God could have simply spoken her into being, but instead, we are told that the woman was taken from within man's body—a rib bone from his side, symbolizing that they would work and love and live together side by side.

In our culture of pitting woman and man against each other, we need to let this sink in: God created woman because man needed her, and she alone, in all the earth, would be a "suitable helper" for him (v. 20). They were created to share the work they had been entrusted with, as well as to share the pleasure and companionship of each other. They were to live in unity as one flesh.

So God performed a little surgery. Every other creature was created from the dust of the earth and spoken into being. But the creation of woman was something different. God caused the man to fall into a deep sleep because apparently the first surgery, performed by God, required the first anesthesia. When Adam awoke, God, acting as Father of the bride, presented her to her groom. Couldn't you just imagine the photographers standing by to capture the perfect photograph of Adam's "first look" at his bride? Finally, we hear Adam speak for the first time. It was a declaration of unity, acknowledging the intimate connection of "bone of my bones and flesh of my flesh" (v. 23).

Then, in one short sentence, we see the establishment of relationships: "For this reason a man will leave his father and mother and be united to his wife" (v. 24). Man and woman would become one flesh because it was "not good for the man to be alone" (v. 18). That was the first time God seemed to think something He had created was less than "good." Everything else, at the end of each day, was declared by Him to be "good." He cared about Adam's "aloneness," so He created someone so very like Adam. She would walk and work alongside him, and together they would become one.

Are you aware that the Lord God, Creator of the universe, cares so very much about us not feeling alone? This story tells us He desires relationship—with us and for us. Adam and Eve's nakedness symbolized having no boundaries between them— nothing held back or hidden. All was right with the world after that first look at the first bride. "You may kiss the bride."

Does this all sound too good to be true? Well, in the telling, we have left out one little clause in the fine print. At the time it seemed a little thing because of all the abundance of good and the almost limitless freedom. But there it is—the "you must not" that we don't like to hear, right there in verse 17: "But you must not eat from the tree of the knowledge of good and evil, for when you eat of it you will surely die." God, in His wisdom and goodness, gave Adam limits, boundaries.

Oh, I take that back—*a* boundary. Just one. In the beginning God gave Adam—before we women ever arrived on the scene—just *one* limit, in the form of a command. And he couldn't even obey that *one*. So why did God give Adam that one boundary? This is important to think about.

There used to be emergency service announcements on television. They were announced with annoying, disruptive buzzing sounds and high-pitched beeps. Over a graphic test pattern, an announcer would come on saying, "This is a test. This is only a test." That idea of "only a test'" makes you think tests are not important—they don't really count. Tests in God's world count. The outcome of the test makes a difference in what follows.

Think about it. Say you needed a knee replacement or a tumor removed from your lung. Would you care if your surgeon had passed or failed the medical tests necessary to become a doctor? What would make you confident in his abilities before he sliced into your skin with a scalpel?

Would you care—would it be important to you—if your child's teacher had failed the tests necessary to earn a teaching degree? "Oh, that was just a test. It didn't really mean anything!" When you are driving on the interstate, aren't you really hoping that all those people in control of the cars traveling seventy miles an hour around you have taken and passed their driver's tests?

Tests are good. Tests establish our intentions. They measure our desires. They reveal the state of our heart.

So here we have a beautiful garden with a man and a woman who were made for each other and for a relationship with their Creator, God, who came to walk and talk with them in the garden in the cool of the day. What could be better? Sounds heavenly, right?

God is good. Do we believe that? Do we trust Him? Do we wish to live in His garden and love His creation? Do we want to share with Him our thoughts and hear His? Are we willing to place our living, breathing lives into His hands—live life by His rules, His boundaries? Or do we have other intentions?

Ah, now that becomes the rest of the story, doesn't it?

3
INTRODUCING SATAN AND HIS LIES
Read Genesis 3

M any years ago I was working on a job with a group of people from LA, and one of the guys found out I was a Christian during a discussion at dinner about reincarnation. You would have thought I had two heads! He seemed both fascinated and repulsed by me, and what followed was hours of conversation spread out over the next two nights. During that time he told me he wanted to get a tattoo on the back of his neck that said *SLAVE*. Now it was my turn to be both fascinated and repulsed! He had no reason or explanation for why he'd chosen that word— and it wasn't until days later that I realized he was exactly right: it was the perfect description with which to define oneself.

Most of us don't realize who or what we are. We walk around thinking we have all this freedom, all these choices we can make—when the truth of the matter is, we are all slaves! The apostle Paul, when writing to Roman Christians, explained that we are either slaves to the sin in our lives, or we have been set free from sin and have become slaves to God—a very good kind of slavery that results in eternal life (Romans 6:6, 22). So my dinner companion was right: the perfect permanent identifying tattoo for him was exactly who and what he was—*SLAVE*.

Well, where did this all start? This whole slavery thing? Let's start at the beginning. In a garden: "Now the serpent was more crafty than any of the wild animals the LORD God had made. He said to the woman, 'Did God *really* say [doubt], "You must not eat from *any tree* [lie] in the garden"?'" (Genesis 3:1, my emphasis).

Now, why did God let the serpent go wandering around in the garden anyway? (Remember, tests are good, tests are good: they establish our intentions.)

Danger! Danger! This one "simple question" from the serpent is loaded with hidden meaning. The serpent is really saying: "I doubt God's honesty, provision, intentions. Don't tell me you are trusting Him?"

"Did God *really* say …?"

Notice how the serpent introduces doubt first and then punctuates it with a lie: "You must not eat from *any tree* in the garden." Although Eve clarifies that it is only one tree that is off limits, she jumps on the exaggeration train and adds *another* rule: "God did say, 'You must not eat fruit from the tree that is in the middle of the garden, *and you must not touch it*, or you will die'" (v. 3, my emphasis).

This is one of the crafty serpent's tricks: If we exaggerate God's boundaries, His rules, then they seem unreasonable and ridiculous. Suddenly God seems like someone who is selfish. He is holding back something *good* from us.

When we doubt God's goodness to us, then we open the door to falling for Satan's beautiful lies. Sure enough, that fruit suddenly became the most desirable thing in the whole wide garden for Eve. It would be tasty and nourishing for food—good for the body. It was pleasing and attractive to look at: eye candy for the soul and spirit. It would give Eve wisdom like no other, so it was also good for the mind. That piece of fruit had it going on—and so she had to have it!

The crafty serpent Satan uses this same line of reasoning today: doubt first, beautiful lies second. He always presents his temptation as an advantage. Always. It always looks like a good thing. It always makes God's wisdom and provision and boundaries look stupid and selfish.

Before sin entered our world, no barriers existed between man and woman and God. When man and woman turned their backs on God by sinning, suddenly they realized they needed a physical barrier of clothing to symbolize the spiritual barrier they had just chosen. So they designed clothes out of fig leaves for themselves as they hid. This was the first act of self-sufficiency, providing for themselves instead of trusting God for their needs.

Then we have the first game of hide-and-seek. The first locked door.

"Where are you?" God, who is good, called out (v. 9). This is the question that an unchanging God still calls out to us: "Where are you?" It's not because He doesn't know or can't see where we are. It's because He wants us to understand, very clearly, the truth of the matter—that He is good. And sin (turning our backs on God) means pain and death.

Today we continue to reply much like Adam did to the question, "Where are you?"

"I am afraid," we answer.

"I am naked," we answer.

"I am hiding," we answer.

We have brought death into ourselves.

It affects our relationship with God because we no longer walk intimately in the garden in the cool of the day, deep in conversation with the Creator.

It affects our relationship with each other, with desire and control battling it out in the ongoing struggle between men and women.

It affects our connection with our bodies since women now experience pain and suffering when bringing new life into the world.

It affects our relationship with the earth we live in because sin ushered in thorns and thistles, and now our work becomes a struggle signified by the sweat on our brow.

We have brought death into our world by trusting Satan's lies instead of God's goodness. We are a people who have chosen sin and continue to face the consequences (3:20–24). Every country, every people group, every age—we choose sin. We make decisions that *we* want to make for ourselves that go against God. We take our stand against a universal understanding of what is right and wrong. We steal from each other, we slander each other, we disrespect and demean each other, we lust, we envy, we lie. We murder our babies, we cheat on our spouses. We forget about God whenever it is convenient. We choose sin.

And we try to cover it with fig leaves. We justify it, ignore it, deny it, push it into the dark. The only thing that can cover our sin—odd as it sounds—is blood. Blood that's shed by innocence: something without blame, without fault, without blemish.

> "Come now, let us reason together, says the LORD:
> though your sins are like scarlet,
> they shall be as white as snow;
> though they are red like crimson,
> they shall become like wool." (Isaiah 1:18 ESV)

Adam and Eve tried to cover themselves and hide their nakedness, their exposure to evil. It didn't work. It took God covering them in animal skins. It took shedding some innocent animal's blood to cover them so they could move forward into life.

It was the beginning of a story that would be continued.

In another garden, the snake would appear again. "Did God *really* say …?" he would begin again. This time the answers would be different. "I lay down My life," would be the answer. The solution would be, "I will shed My blood. I will offer My flesh. I will be the sacrificial lamb."

A man named Jesus did what we could not do. He defeated the crafty serpent, crushing his head, destroying his plans of eternal pain and death, and forever covering our sins with His holy and innocent blood.

Jesus talked about our slavery to sin to people who took offense at His words. His conversation was with Israelites who had no memory of being slaves but considered themselves as chosen by God as His own. They came from a long heritage of following God, covering their sins with their good works and their sacrifices. Jesus told them: "You cannot hear My words because you can only hear your father's lies. But if you can hear—and hold onto My teaching—then you can know the truth, and that truth will set you free" (John 8:31–47, my paraphrase).

Satan and his lies or God and His truth: Which will you hold on to? Are you a slave to your sin and its bondage? Or are you a slave to God and His freedom? Whose voice are you listening to? As you walk along the path in the garden, who will you trust?

4
SIN CROUCHES AT YOUR DOOR
Read Genesis 4–6:8

As a child, I grew up spending every Sunday afternoon at my grandparents' house. It was already an old white farmhouse when my grandparents had moved into it as newly-weds, and they had raised their three children there amid crops of cotton and old barns and lifelong neighbors.

I loved looking at their old black-and-white photographs, most of them taken in the 1940s, with dates and names inked on the bottom edge of the border in my aunt's cursive hand. I especially loved staring into the young face of my dad, hair dark and curly, a shy grin, standing beside his older brother, who was a little taller and a lot more confident. Both incredibly handsome, hanging out in the front yard with high school friends or dressed in uniform with their buddies in France.

My uncle was four years older than my dad, but they seemed to be almost inseparable. They had stories of growing up together and they were completely, totally connected with each other's lives. Unfortunately, for complicated reasons, my grandfather—a very stately, soft-spoken man—left my father as executor of his will when he died, and my uncle's part of the inheritance skipped him and went to his two sons instead. My father, the younger brother, oversaw the estate. This did not sit well with my uncle, whose anger slowly burned deeper and deeper until he would no longer speak to my dad. And it tore my dad apart.

Within a few years of my grandfather passing away, my dad suffered a heart attack, which caused a stroke. The stroke destroyed his ability to talk and read and write, and then unbelievably he was diagnosed with a malignant, fatal brain tumor. With all of this, the most palpable heartbreak was that his brother, his best friend, with whom he had shared his life, would no longer talk to him.

One day as I drove home from Atlanta to Greenville, I became convinced if I went to talk to my uncle, I could get him to understand how sick my daddy was and how stupid this whole thing was. I hoped that I could convince him to go the few miles across town to see my dad and talk to him before he died.

I drove straight to his house and knocked on the back door, heart pounding. He was delighted to see me and led me through his house that was so familiar to me, back to the kitchen. So there I was, sitting at my uncle's kitchen table, with tears streaming down my face, pleading with him to see my dad—to see his brother one last time.

Pride is a poisonous thing. Even now I can still see my uncle, his eyes wild, his face red, his finger jabbing at the air because "my *baby brother* has control of *my inheritance*—money that was rightfully mine—and *no*, I will not do it. I will not see my brother. It's mine, I tell you, and he, *my baby brother*, will not let me have it."

It's an old story. It's as old as Cain and Abel. We will see it again in Jacob and Esau, and Joseph and his older brothers. You probably have a similar story floating around in your closet. Some stories don't have a happy ending. We wish they did. We wish we could understand why things happen. We wish that we could justify them, reason them out. We wish that our tears could make them better. But that is not what we see in this difficult world around us. It's just not.

We look at this story of Cain and Abel, with God's acceptance of one brother's offering and lack of acceptance of the other, and we ask, "Why, God? Why didn't You accept both?" There may be hints of the attitudes of their hearts in the giving: the older brother gave some of his crops while the younger brother gave from the first and the best of his livestock—the valuable fat of the firstborn calf. It is a challenge, isn't it? What am I holding back from God that He desires? What betrays my heart? What tells the story of my selfishness? What do I refuse to give that tells God that I do not trust Him?

That is why we need God so desperately: God asking us questions so that we confront our actions. God coming to us, hand extended, inviting us to do the right thing. God warning us not to go down that path of pride and jealousy. God cautioning us not to hold so tightly to our self-righteous anger. It is crouching at our door. It desires to have us.

God, who is righteous and good, cannot ignore our choice of wrong. The blood we spill in our anger cries out to Him. He cannot allow the unrepentant to continue living in our home, poisoning the air. As God said to Cain, "You have destroyed your brother. You must leave. You must wander. The very dirt you came from will no longer welcome you home"

(Genesis 4:10–12, my paraphrase). So Cain left his family to form his own, and they wandered, set apart.

Death entered the world from man's own hands. Who saw that coming back there in that garden of delights? Cain murdered, then denied it. There was no repentance. No "I am sorry! Look at what I have done!" There was no bringing it out into the light so he could have been forgiven. There was only fear of death: "Someone may do to me what I did to my own brother!" (v. 14, my paraphrase). And we see God's incredible kindness: "I will place my mark of protection on you—so that no one will harm you" (v. 15, my paraphrase).

We follow Cain and his family for a while—just long enough to see the beginning of a pattern: like father, like son. It doesn't take long for his family line to take the stand of Cain: "I have murdered another and I declare myself immune to punishment," Lamech said (vv. 23–24, my paraphrase). This thinking would continue and become epidemic. Cain and his descendants chose a path of death. It was a path that took them further and further away from God.

It is subtle, and you might have missed it, but look back. In the beginning, God said, "Let us make man in *our* image" (1:26). After the fall from God's grace, men had children in *their own* image (5:3). God is spirit. Humans are flesh. There is a conflict there between the two—and this will be the continuing battle. God's desire is for us to be born of His Spirit, to look more like Him. Our very human desire of the flesh is to satisfy ourselves, to keep our eyes focused on me alone. That, my friend, is where everything starts falling apart. This will be the theme song from Genesis to Revelation: choosing God's spirit of righteousness or satisfying our own desires of the flesh. We have all met the toddler, fist raised defiantly into the air, declaring, "I do it myself!" And how often we choose that way ourselves!

Life outside of Eden has been harder than Adam and Eve could have imagined. Their death from eating of the tree of good and evil was not quick enough; it was slow and painful. God had given them two sons, and by the end of Genesis 4, both have been lost to them. But in His graciousness, He gave them another son to trace forward: Seth. As we follow this line along, we see two interesting themes: they have incredibly long lives, producing many children, and they all have the same ending—they die. Except for one: Enoch.

Genesis 5 gives an interesting description for this man: "Enoch walked with God," and instead of dying, "he was no more, because God took him away" (v. 24). We can also read a little about him in the letter written to the Hebrews (11:5), where it commends his faith, and in the book written by Jesus's half brother Jude (1:14–15).

Jude wrote a fiery letter to warn of godless men—as in men and women who don't walk *with* God but have chosen their own path instead. They are "grumblers and faultfinders; they follow their own evil desires" (1:16). They are "autumn trees, without fruit and uprooted—twice dead" (v. 12). They have "taken the way of Cain" (v. 11). Jude even threw into the mix of the godless those "angels who did not keep their positions of authority but abandoned their home" (v. 6). Then Jude contrasted the godless with one who walked with God—Enoch, the seventh descendant from Adam, who prophesied about the future of those who do not walk with God: "See, the Lord is coming with thousands upon thousands of his holy ones to judge everyone, and to convict [declare guilty] all of them of the ungodly acts they have committed in their ungodliness" (vv. 14–15 NIV 2011).[2]

Outside the Garden of Eden, it didn't take long for folks to start deciding either to walk with God or walk their own path without Him. "Be on guard," God warned Cain, "sin is crouching at your door, walking with you along your path, and it longs to have you" (Genesis 4:7, my paraphrase). Once we have started out on our own path, separate from God, it is difficult to fight off the enemy who walks beside our path always looking for an opening to attack us.

It is chilling to read so soon into the story of humanity that God has grown weary of hearing the death cries of His children. "I can hear it no longer," He says. "I will wipe them from the face of the earth, for I am grieved that I have made them" (6:7, my paraphrase).

Could the story really end so soon? Given the choice, do we always choose our own way? Is it really so hard to walk the path with God (v. 9)? Would God really grow so weary of us? What are we to do? Who can possibly save us from ourselves?

5
TRUSTING THE SHIPBUILDER
Read Genesis 6–9:17

Hanging over my desk is a beautiful framed print depicting the final outcome of Noah's ark. It is a picture that children would love with blue skies at the top and blue water below, birds flying high, and dolphins and swans swimming merrily along the surface of the sea. Animals crisscross brown sandy mountains two by two as they parade down to the shore. At the top of the mountain, the ark sits at a jaunty angle as Noah and his wife watch the remaining ostriches, chickens, and goats make their way down the ramp. Three men on the deck look on, almost as if they wished they could wave goodbye to the friends they're leaving behind.

Noah's ark. It is the story children love to imagine.

I have read that almost every culture has a "great flood" story. I find this fascinating, especially if you scan through them and start seeing the strangest similarities: the water coming from rain above and springs below, the building of an ark or finding a boat (or an acorn!) so that just one man and often his three sons and their families can ride out the storm, along with animals, often two by two, who are also in for the wild ride. In some stories the waters rain down for seven days; in others, the water covers the earth for a year and birds are sent out to establish that the ground is dry again. In almost all of them, mankind had become wicked, and their god (whatever he is named) could stand it no longer.[3] For me, the pure universal nature of this story gives it credibility. It becomes more than children's entertainment. It starts to sound a bit more like world history to me. So that is the way I will approach it.

The Hebrew account we find in Genesis is a story punctuated with numbers. We have the exact dimensions of the ark. Translating the Hebrew measurements into English, it is a giant boat, measuring 450 feet long, 75 feet wide, and 45 feet high—and then add a roof and a covering, leaving 18 inches of opening all around at the top, which I am hoping is for light and ventilation. It is the height of a modern three-story building with three interior decks. Nothing matching its size was built until the mid-nineteenth century. Modern engineering will tell you that it would be incredibly stable in turbulent seas, and our modern-day aircraft carriers are similar in proportion.[4]

The exact days and dates are even given. Specifically, the great springs beneath the earth burst forth on the seventeenth day of the second month in Noah's six hundredth year (7:11). It rained for forty days and forty nights, lifting the ark to more than twenty feet above the top of the mountains. The water flooded for one hundred fifty days. On the seventeenth day of the seventh month, the ark came to rest on Mount Ararat, and on the first day of the tenth month, the tops of the mountains became visible (8:4–5). By the twenty-seventh day of the second month in the following year (okay, that's over a year now!), the earth was completely dry, and God called for Noah and his family to come out.

The biblical account is like a journal entry filled with specific, factual details. In reality, it is a traveler's log kept through the adventure of a lifetime. I must say, though, that it is more than that: it is the story of one believing man's journey with God. A journey based on impossible faith, total trust, against all logical reason, flying in the face of cultural norms. Noah must have seemed like a lunatic! How do you get to a faith like that?

I love the description of Noah we read in the Bible: "a righteous man, blameless among the people of his time, and he walked with God" (6:9). Wouldn't you love to get that description attached to your name?

It seems that Noah just nodded his head, gathered the wood, built the ark, and then slathered on the pitch to make sure everything was watertight inside and out. He didn't check the forecast first or see what his neighbors thought before heading out to build a ship on dry land. God said it, and he did it. I ask again, how do you get a faith like that?

Noah was given quite an insurmountable task to do. Wouldn't you have been overwhelmed? The enormity of building the ark; gathering the animals two by two, some by seven; and then the food supply to last who knows how long? We are told simply that "Noah did everything just as God commanded him" (6:22; see also 7:5).

We also find two sweet gestures on God's part within the task of packing everything up. First, Noah didn't have to take off on a safari to round all the animals up—they came to him. Second, they entered the ark all by themselves. Wouldn't that have been a wonderful thing to see? I think that is such a true picture of God and His graciousness. I would have been fretting about how to find and then coax the antelope on board, but God simply had them show up on their own and prance right on in the door, settling quietly down next to their neighbors.

In Matthew 10:29–31, God tells us that He knows the number of hairs on our head and He cares for the sparrows, and we are not to hold onto worry or let it haunt us. Still, so often we look at the looming mountains ahead in our lives and worry how we will ever get around them, even though God may have our path take a sharp turn in another direction before we ever get there. Ah, how kind God was to Noah—and how kind He is to us!

The ark must have had a massive doorway—tall enough to accommodate the giraffe's tall neck, and a platform strong enough to support a pair of elephants. Speaking of the giant door, we also find a lovely detail as the rains began to fall: God Himself shut them in, safe and sound (Genesis 7:16). Noah and his family and all the creatures with them floated warm and dry while enclosed in the ark of God.

Hush now. Do you hear the rain coming down upon the roof? It was the first recorded time for it to fall from the heavens. Do you hear the "whoosh" of water rushing from the depths of the ground—the water that God had built land on in the beginning, those streams that watered Eden from below?

Outside the protection of the ark, only God could see the destruction of His precious world. Three anguished sentences tell the story:

> Every living thing that moved on the earth per-
> ished—birds, livestock, wild animals, all the crea-
> tures that swarm over the earth, and all mankind.
> Everything on dry land that had the breath of life
> in its nostrils died. Every living thing on the face of
> the earth was wiped out; men and animals and the
> creatures that move along the ground and the birds
> of the air were wiped from the earth. (vv. 21–23)

We must look back at this good God and see what caused Him to destroy the very things that had brought Him joy in creating.

Genesis 6:5–6 tells us that the Lord was grieved at how great man's wickedness had become—grieved that He had created man on earth because the thoughts of his heart were evil all the time. The Lord's heart was filled with pain because man's heart was filled with evil. We never think of that, do we? We don't think of the Lord God feeling pain when He sees the evil we nurture in our own hearts. It is a pain so deep and sear-ing that He no longer walks with us in the cool of the evening but chooses to wipe us from the face of the earth instead.

Pause.

Let it sober you. Suddenly we are seeing a very different picture of our God. This is not the God of children's bedtime stories. This is the God of judgment.

The great flood was judgment, pure and simple. There were those who turned away from God, embracing the evil in their hearts every moment of every day. There were also a very few, a handful, who said yes to shipbuilding—believing God when He said the water would come and flood the earth.

Turn and look at this God who cares about the state of your heart. He is terrifying and mighty. He is tender and loving. He is Creator. He is Lord God. He is Judge of good and evil. Do you see it now? He is not warm milk to pacify the babies. He is not a nagging voice to be ignored. He is not a manifestation of imagination. He is a judge who knows the difference between what is good and what is evil. Like the water that rained down from above and burst forth from the deep, He will destroy the evil that breaks His heart. Or He will save the good that turns to listen to His voice and walk in His ways.

Judge and judgment—we have learned a new thing about our God.

"But God remembered Noah ... and the waters receded" (8:1). You, like Noah, might find yourself in the perfect storm, not of your own making. The tempest is raging around you, the ship is rocking, and the animals need to be fed. But He's got you. He has placed you safely inside that waterproof ark until the rain stops falling and the waters subside. Trust Him. Trust His protection. Trust His timing. Soon He will send the dove holding the olive branch of restored peace. Soon God will call you out of the ark of protection and place your feet on dry ground. The storm will pass. In the meantime, you are cupped in His hands.

After leaving the ark Noah's first response was worship (v. 20). Ah, now we understand the inclusion of the seven "clean animals and birds" (7:2–3). Some of them were to be a blood sacrifice for a burnt offering to God—their Savior who saved them from the destruction of the floodwaters. The aroma of Noah's offering was sweet to the Lord (8:21). He made a promise in His heart—a promise that He shared with Noah and his sons and every living creature. It was a promise, a covenant for all generations to come: "Never again will the waters become a flood to destroy all life" (9:11, my paraphrase).

Water is a powerful force. Look at the biblical stories featuring water after Noah's time. A baby would be hidden on the waters of the Nile River, floating along in a basket coated with tar and pitch. An Egyptian princess would find him, and he would be named Moses, meaning "I drew him out of the water" (Exodus 2:1–10).

Later, as the Egyptian army pursued the Israelites, this same Moses would lead God's people up to the edge of another body of water: the Red Sea. With a strong east wind God would part the waters to allow them to safely pass on dry ground to the other side, and then bring the waters back together to destroy their enemy (Exodus 14).

After the death of Moses, Joshua would lead the nation of Israel out of the desert to the entrance to the Promised Land: the floodwaters of the Jordan River. As soon as the priests carrying the ark of the Lord would step into the water, the water upstream would stop flowing, and they would pass safely through the waters and into the Promised Land (Joshua 3).

Time and again, then, God carried His people through the water!

Hundreds of years later a man would appear in the desert crying out for repentance and a return to the path of the Lord. His name was John, and he offered a baptism of water, signifying a new life—likely doing most of his baptizing in the very same Jordan River that Joshua and the Israelites crossed.

Then another man would come behind John claiming to be the Life that was in the water. He would explain to a woman who had chosen evil that He alone could give her living water and that it would well up from within her so that she would never be thirsty again. Indeed, it would be a spring of eternal life (John 4:4–14). He would also proclaim to the masses this same message of finding streams of living water in Him by way of the Spirit who would come after His ascension (7:37–39).

Water. It is a powerful force God used for judgment and destruction in the time of Noah, and it broke His heart. From that time on, though, He would use water as a sign of His deliverance. To submit to His "washing" was to walk in His path of forgiveness—to accept His salvation.

We even find this promise in Isaiah 43:2–3:

> "When you go through deep waters,
>   I will be with you.
> When you go through rivers of difficulty,
>   you will not drown.
> When you walk through the fire of oppression,
>   you will not be burned up;
>   the flames will not consume you.
> For I am the LORD, your God,
>   the Holy One of Israel, your Savior." (NLT)

After the waters of the great flood had receded, God gave us—and every creature on earth—a sign for all time. It is His bow of light: "I have set my rainbow in the clouds, and it will be the sign of the covenant [the promise] between me and the earth" (Genesis 9:13). Although people take such signs of God and change the meaning for their own agenda, we know the true significance of this rainbow of light stretching across God's heavens after the rain. It is a promise of deliverance instead of destruction. It is there for all of us as a promise. It is there for God as a reminder. The rainbow is God's sign that He will remember His covenant, His promise to us.

But the world that God had created was changed with the flood. With God's original charge to increase in number and fill the earth came new rules to the game. Fear now entered between humans and the beasts of the earth and the birds of the air. Suddenly we were allowed to eat animals as food. But God commanded humanity not to eat meat that has the life force of their blood still in it and that we must carefully drain it from the flesh of the animals before eating their meat. Interesting—blood becomes something very important in this scheme of life and death. Life is declared sacred. The animals are held accountable to God, and humans are held accountable to God because man is created in God's image. To kill man is to harm God, and the penalty is the life of the one who kills.

God hits the Reset button and the world starts anew. It starts anew, yes, but it is not utopia. We have seen how fragile life can be, and we have had a glimpse of judgment. We are a long way from the Garden of Eden, and the mud is still squishing between our toes. Something tells me that other storm clouds loom ahead.

The question we must ask ourselves is, Can we trust the Shipbuilder when the rain begins to fall?

6
NOAH AND NAMES
Read Genesis 9–11

A few years ago my husband, Jeff, asked me, "Will you take a ride with me?"

"Where are we going?" I asked.

"I'm not going to tell you," he said. "It's a secret."

"I'm in."

So off we went. We drove past all his usual haunts—and I was silently trying to figure out where we were going. Finally, we pulled into a cemetery next to a church in Lilburn. I would come to find out later that area was once a little community known as Luxomni.

My husband's last name has an unusual spelling (I kid him and tell him that's why I didn't take his last name when we married). But our kids have his last name, so I still end up spelling it out or saying it with the explanation: "Mathews with one *t*."

My husband had found a cemetery with graves from the 1800s with a family that had both spellings: one *t* and two—so you had a father with the last name of "Matthews" and his infant son with the last name of "Mathews." (So obviously I was wise not to take my husband's misspelled name!) Well, these two families named Mathews and Matthews turned out to be relatives of his. Not only that, they were the link that led him to the grave of his great-great-great-grandfather who was buried at the next church a mile down the road. All this was really interesting because he had no idea his family ever lived in Georgia (everyone he knew of was in Alabama)—much less within thirty miles of our Atlanta home.

One other thing about our little cemetery adventure: In that same graveyard with the Mathews with one *t* and two, we also found some Cunninghams. Now Cunningham is *my* mother's maiden name—and all the family I knew of lived in South Carolina. But there they were: the Cunninghams and the misspelled Mathewses all living together in the same small community, going to the same church, parading about in their Sunday best 150 years ago.

Well, even with that kind of family name background in my own life, as I started reading through Genesis 9–11 and came across all these unfamiliar names, my eyes glazed over. *Ugh, how boring*, I thought. *This just does not mean anything to me.* But then I glanced at the cross-references listed in the middle column of each page in my Bible. I couldn't believe how many scriptural references related to those names! I slowly started understanding that those names were—and are—meaningful. The Hebrew people who originally heard those names would have been thinking, *Oh! That was my great-great-uncle.* Or, *I knew them! They were a powerful influence in our village.* Or, *Yes! That was that contentious, competitive man whose family became our enemy!*

It would be like us saying, "I come from the Kennedy family." You get a picture in your head of money and privilege and political power. Or, "I am a descendant of Picasso." You suddenly think of a fascinating, brilliant, prolific artist. Think of other famous last names: Rembrandt, Du Pont, Vanderbilt, or even Hitler. Those family names mean something—they define who you are and what has influenced you. They give you identity.

What we come to understand about God as we read His Word is that He not only made us in His image, but He also knows and cares about us. Even more interesting, He created us with a purpose—a purpose that fits into a great plan. He tells us clearly that we are not accidental—nor are we accidentally here right now in this specific place and time.

I love the following passage, which is part of a message given by the Hebrew Paul as recorded in the Acts of the Apostles:

> The God who made the world and everything in it
> is the Lord of heaven and earth and does not live in
> temples built by human hands. And he is not served
> by human hands, as if he needed anything. Rather, he
> himself gives everyone life and breath and everything
> else. From one man he made all the nations, that they
> should inhabit the whole earth; and he marked out
> their appointed times in history and the boundaries of
> their lands. God did this so that they would seek him
> and perhaps reach out for him and find him, though
> he is not far from any one of us. (17:24–27 NIV 2011)

God created this earth, and everyone in it, with a great plan. We are all connected from the beginning. He placed us exactly here and exactly at this time. This is the mystery of God! From one man, He made all the nations that would inhabit the whole earth. We cannot begin to comprehend it. Here we have this God of mercy preserving the line of Adam through Noah and his family, blessing them, and sending them out into the world to multiply and inhabit the land. God gives them an awareness of purpose and an understanding of the importance of family relationships, writing down their bloodlines as the generations unfold.

They will mess up along the way. Unfortunately, they do so immediately, with this odd little story included here of Noah drinking too much wine and passing out in his tent without his clothes on. *Seriously*, I think to myself, *did God really need to record this sad story for us?* I want to ignore it, and not think about it at all. But here it is, included in this history of God and His people. It is the story of shame that Noah brings upon himself. And it is the story of how his three sons react. One son draws attention to his father's shame, two sons cover his shame with a garment, reminding us of God covering the nakedness of Adam and Eve with a garment made of skin. Noah awakens the next day to bless two of his sons and curse one. He lives 950 years and dies. His sons prosper and multiply and everyone seems to go merrily along their way until they start up a little building project around the next bend in the road.

Before that happens, we pause here to jump into the family tree of Noah branching out into clans and becoming nations. These stories of names and nations explain who the sons and grandsons and great-grandsons of Noah were and where they settled and by what names their tribes were called, stretching from Egypt to Asia. These names and nations will reappear as we continue our journey through the centuries, especially the names of the tribes of Canaan, descendants of Ham. However, we will follow the descendants of Shem since these are the Holy Scriptures of the Hebrews. Shem will become the father of the Semites: and we will soon meet one of his descendants, the Hebrew Abram.

I find it interesting how the stories of the New Testament rest on these stories of Genesis. You can find another list of family names stretching back to Adam in Luke's Gospel (3:23–38). A man named Jesus will come to save what was broken in the tent of Noah, and before that in the Garden of Eden. This Jesus will come as Messiah for the Hebrew people and as Savior for the whole world. He will be the garment to cover the shame of the descendants of Shem and Japheth and Ham. He will trace his bloodline through Shem to Noah, reaching back to Adam, the son of God. Names are important to God. Because each one of us is incredibly important to God.

Our God knows each person's name. Our God is detailed, factual, and intentional in His storytelling. All this history and genealogy places a framework around His story: "This is real," He tells us. "This is factual. These were actual people who lived and breathed and walked this earth, and their lives mattered. I have written it down so you will know it is important to Me."

I like that names are important to God. I like that *my* name is important to God. He also tells us that, beyond the Bible, there are *other* important books with names. King David said there was a "book of life" in which the righteous are listed (Psalm 69:28). The apostle Paul also referred to a "book of life" that contained the names of his fellow workers in the gospel (Philippians 4:3). Later John, in his vision, told of books being opened on a day of judgment (Revelation 13:8; 17:8; 20:12–15; 21:27).

If you call yourself by the name of Christ, a Christian, then Jesus promised to acknowledge the names listed in the book of life in front of His Father and the angels: "All who are victorious will be clothed in white. I will never erase their names from the book of life, but I will announce before my Father and his angels that they are mine" (3:5 NLT). Our names are important! They have importance beyond our earthly lifetime. We are told that books will be opened, and our names will be called out on the day of judgment.

So what does this mean, all these books filled with lists of names? It means that starting from the beginning of time to the very last moment a human being takes a breath on this earth, God cares about each person. We are important to Him. He knows our names. He knows us. Perhaps the important thing to ask ourselves is: Do *we* know *Him*?

7
GOD AND WORDS
Read Genesis 11:1–9

We know many of the Genesis stories from Sunday school: Adam and Eve, Cain and Abel, Noah and the ark, the tower of Babel, and others. We have seen that things did not seem to be going along according to plan for the Creator. Things continued to get messy whenever those humans started making their own plans. So let's do a quick review and see where we are.

God, who is good, created man and woman, who rebelled against Him. Their descendants became so evil and self-centered that the only solution was to destroy everything and start over. Then came the flood, with a big wooden boat rocking around on the surface, containing a family and enough animals to begin again. On dry land, salvation complete, God reinstated His love and commitment to them with a rainbow of color—and marching orders. So with instructions in hand to "be fruitful and increase in number and fill the earth" (Genesis 9:1), what did they do?

Yes, you guessed it: Once again they rebelled against God. With childlike defiance, they ignored God's direction to move outward into the whole earth, and instead they clenched their little fists and said, "You can't tell me what to do!"

They rejected God's plan in favor of their own plan. "We will build a great city! We will take pride in our own accomplishments! We will build a tower that reaches up to our own version of 'spirituality'!" (11:3–4, my paraphrase).

This reminds me of an interesting billboard advertising campaign I once heard about. Concerned by how easily we ignore God, a wealthy businessman commissioned the Smith Agency in Florida to create these ads in 1999, and they launched nationwide by the Outdoor Advertising Association of America as a public service. The purpose of the billboards was to remind us, as we speed along the interstate rushing from one thing to the next, that maybe we should give a thought to God.[5]

You probably have seen these black billboards with white type and their very simple one-liners as if spoken by God:

"Why don't you come by my house on Sunday before the game?" God

"Loved the wedding, invite me to the marriage." God

"What part of 'Thou shalt not …' didn't you understand?" God

"Have you read my #1 bestseller? There will be a test." God

Then there is the one that many parents have probably heard themselves say to their own unruly children: *"Don't make me come down there."* God [6]

Well, apparently God did have to come down here in Genesis 11. In the story of the tower of Babel, we certainly see God's sense of humor. Their building project—this tower of Babel—was so big in their eyes but so small in His that he had to figuratively get up and come down here to see it for Himself. It was like He said, "Look at what they are up to now!" and then shook His head in disbelief.

I hope you are starting to understand God's love of the spoken word. God spoke the world into being. In the story of Noah's drunken episode after the flood, his son Ham spoke to his brothers disrespectfully against their father and received punishment for it. Now we hear these descendants of the flood arrogantly ignoring God's word to "be fruitful and increase in number and fill the earth," so God scrambles *their* words. In the blink of an eye, multiple languages are born, making communication among them impossible, and they find themselves scattered all over the earth. Whew! You better watch what you say!

God is not opposed to building cities or towers or joining together for the good of mankind. But He is opposed to us ignoring His plan and substituting our own self-centered ideas.

God's plans are greater than our plans. Are we spending our days—our short, specific, unique time on this great big earth—depending on God, or are we too busy building little nests of self-sufficiency for ourselves? Are we looking to God for all we need, or do we think we can build our own little towers by ourselves?

God tells us words are powerful. To whom do I bring honor with my words—myself or my God? Words are important to God. Choose yours carefully.

8
TRAVELING WITH THE LORD OF THE UNIVERSE
Read Genesis 12–13

Have you ever taken a trip with someone you don't know? A few years ago I needed to take a day trip for work from Atlanta down to Miami. I was told that it had been decided it would be a great opportunity for me to get to know a new marketing rep who had just started working with our company. I was a little hesitant because it's one thing to meet someone over coffee or lunch, but an all-day trip felt a little intense. Yet I really didn't have any say, so this woman I had never met before picked me up at 5:00 a.m. for our 7:30 flight, and off we went.

During that fourteen-hour day, we went from surface chit-chat to deeper conversations about marriage, religion, failed jobs, and raising children. We shared meals, entered unfamiliar situations for work, shopped together, got lost driving our rental car, and eventually found our way back to the Miami airport. If you had seen us sitting in the very last row of the plane on our way back to Atlanta, with our heads close together as we talked, you would have assumed we were very close, dear friends.

Traveling together—especially into foreign or unknown lands (whether Miami or Canaan)—can make for a quick relationship. God, the Lord of the universe, invited a man named Abram to head out on a little road trip with him—a little mystery tour, so to speak. God said, "Leave, Abram. Leave everything familiar—your country, your people, your father's household—and go to somewhere you don't know, somewhere you will always be a stranger. Go to the land I will show you" (Genesis 12:1, my paraphrase). That last line is the key: See, this was the allure of the invitation—the Lord of the universe was going to be traveling with Abram.

God often calls us out of where we are to get our attention and teach us that He can lead us, that He is trustworthy and reliable, and that He is much bigger than our surroundings or the people around us.

Amazingly, they took off together—this man named Abram and God. Right off the bat, Abram decides not to follow God exactly, but to sort of wing it and make his own decisions. There was a famine in the land, so instead of asking God about his dinner plans, he headed to Egypt, where there was food. But there he found Pharaoh and his harem, and suddenly Abram was lying to protect himself: insisting that his beautiful wife Sarai was not his wife, but his sister. The next thing you know, she was dressed in designer clothes and living in the Pharaoh's mansion, and Abram was getting rich in the world of high finance and trading stocks and bonds on Wall Street. If you know anything at all about God, you can probably guess that this was not what He had in mind when he called Abram out to join Him on this little road trip.

So the Lord did a marvelous thing. He inflicted serious diseases on Pharaoh and everyone in his household—except, I assume, Sarai. Pharaoh couldn't get Sarai and her lying husband Abram out of there fast enough: "Take your stuff and head on out the door, please," I imagine him saying.

We might cringe at this detour of Abram's and say, "Boy, he sure got off easy! God didn't even slap him on the hand. And he blatantly lied!" This is more of a picture of God and His goodness than Abram and his deceitfulness. Even when we mess up and get off track, God does not.

This picture of God is beautifully described in an old hymn telling of His faithfulness. Even when we turn our backs on God, He continues to be faithful to us. Even when we doubt Him, He continues to provide for us. God loves us, protects us, and acts on our behalf, even when we lose faith. Great is His faithfulness, indeed.[7]

The next thing you know, Abram and his nephew Lot were back in the Promised Land of Canaan. But then they faced a modern problem—they had too much stuff! They had sheep, cattle, donkeys, camels, menservants, maidservants, silver, gold, and tents (see Genesis 12:16; 13:2, 5). God's blessings had rained down on them, and now they had too much stuff and not enough room. The people they were responsible for—their hired help—started arguing with each other, leading to discord. To make things even worse, those godless neighbors (the Canaanites and Perizzites) were watching all this go on as if it was the local afternoon soap opera.

Abram did something that put him in the top of the class in leadership decision-making. First, he acknowledged the problem instead of ignoring it and hoping it would just work itself out on its own. The second thing he did was go to see Lot with a reasonable solution: "Let's part company" (13:9). Then, amazingly, he selflessly gave Lot—his young nephew (who seems to be a bit of a hanger-on)—the first choice of land.

Now Lot could have looked to the north or to the south and chosen from a 150-mile stretch of land. But instead, Lot looked east toward the cities of Sodom and Gomorrah—cities filled with wickedness and idolatry. This was the pivotal situation that put Abram on one course and sent Lot in a very different direction. As time went on, Lot drew closer and closer to a life separated from God. Eventually, through Abram's prayers, God sent angels to physically pull Lot and his family out of harm's way. But Abram continued to talk with the Lord and began to reflect on the generous, peace-loving God he was traveling with.

With Abram's journey starting in Ur and moving on to Haran and Shechem, Bethel and Hebron, we see an interesting picture of who God is. He is personal. He spoke to Abram very specifically, very one-on-one. Look at how Abram responded: with reverence and awe as he built altars and bowed down to worship Him. And God revealed Himself to Abram as a God of promises. His ongoing promise was and continues to be that to anyone who would draw close to Him, He would provide for them throughout eternity. The promise He made to Abram is no little promise. Listen:

> "I will make you into a great nation
>   [a unified people]
> and I will bless you [prosperity];
> I will make your name great
>   [reputation, powerful influence],
> and you will be a blessing
>   [you will bring prosperity to others]." (12:2)

Yikes! What a contrast to those people building the tower of Babel to make a name for themselves! He continued:

> "I will bless those who bless you
>   [profitable, powerful relationships],
> and whoever curses you I will curse [protection];
> And all peoples on earth
> will be blessed through you." (v. 3)

Read that again: "*all* peoples." Reminder here: one of Abram's descendants was David, and one of David's descendants was Jesus. I think that is the blessing we are talking about here.

We will pause here, with Abram standing there, looking out into this land where God has led him. Again God talked with him:

> "Look up. Look north and south and east and west.
> All the land you see I will give you and your descendants forever. Your descendants (oh, yes, you with no children!) will be as numerous as the dust of the earth you see before you—uncountable! Come,

let's walk this land together—so you can see it,
touch it, experience it, and know that it is real—and
that I am real. And we will be traveling together."
(13:14–17, my paraphrase)

Have you ever felt God leading you away from what was
familiar and into a new land of unknowns? Are you willing to
trust God as your tour guide through this life? If your answer
is yes, something tells me it will be one heck of an adventure!

9
I PLEDGE ALLEGIANCE TO THE LORD
Read Genesis 14

When I was in grade school, our class would stand after the bell each morning. Every child turned and faced the flag—the American flag—that stood in the corner on its little stand. We placed our hands over our hearts, and we said in unison, "I pledge allegiance to the Flag of the United States of America, and to the Republic for which it stands, one Nation under God, indivisible, with liberty and justice for all."

Unfortunately our "Pledge of Allegiance" causes controversy in this day and age—and actually, it has from its inception in the 1800s. Complaints came from religious groups who saw it as idolatry, or from patriots who felt that the original salute to the flag looked too much like the Nazi salute of the Germans. In a country founded on freedom, some people did not want to be told they had to stand or salute or do or say anything they didn't want to.[8]

I was raised in a family where military service was common. My mother was an army nurse in World War II. Her husband, the father of my two older sisters, gave his life serving his country in Korea after also serving in WWII. My dad and his brother, and all my uncles who were of fighting age, served in WWII. My dear neighbor across the street, Dave Castles, spent several years as a prisoner of war in Germany after his plane went down behind enemy lines. I grew up with a generation before me that was willing to sacrifice their very lives for their country. Because of this, I am very comfortable, and actually very proud, to swear an oath of allegiance to this country I live in. I am grateful for the freedom and protection that I enjoy because of the allegiance of so many to this country.

The word "allegiance" means "devotion or loyalty to a person, group, or cause."[9] The original Latin of the related word "ally" means "to bind to."[10]

In this fourteenth chapter of Genesis, we read about many countries that joined forces. I have a good bit of trouble trying to keep all the tribal names and their kings straight. If you want a simplified overview of this passage, it divides easily into two camps. In the first camp were two alliances of various kings in the region, and these two alliances went to war with each other. Abram's nephew Lot, in choosing to live within the boundaries of one of those countries, had thus allied himself with this camp—simply by living there with the people of Sodom. This ended up getting Lot into a *lot* of trouble (sorry, couldn't resist the pun). And this was just the beginning of Lot's troubles.

The other camp consisted of a couple of "outsiders," who seemed to ally themselves with God alone: our friend Abram and a mysterious man named Melchizedek who had formed his own allegiance with the One he called "God Most High" (vv. 18–20).

How does this story teach us anything beyond tribal conflict among warring nations? All we see on the surface are multiple nations in an alliance, conquering and being conquered, with the spoils of war divided and Lot being dragged off into captivity. Let's concentrate on the two men who refused to form even a vague, subtle alliance with a person, a king, or a country. They seemed to understand the importance of choosing the right alliance because of how it would direct their paths and affect their lives. Let's look at the actions of Abram, and let's look at the presence of this man named Melchizedek. I am sure God has an amazing reason for telling us this small story.

One reason for alliances in any period of history is simply protection from each other. I have trouble relating to this passage of warring nations, of being conquered or defeated by enemies, because I have never experienced war. My generation's experience of the 9-11 attacks is as close as it has gotten. Most of us in America have lived peacefully sleeping in our beds, knowing all is safe and sound around us. Recently, I ate dinner with a German woman. As we talked, casually getting to know each other, she told me she didn't know who her mother's father was—her own grandfather—because when her grandmother was a young girl, she had been raped by Russian soldiers. I felt like ice water had suddenly been thrown into my face. For her, though, it was an everyday reality.

That is reality, then and now, for many people throughout our world. It is not uncommon for bigger, stronger countries to come in and take over their smaller, weaker neighbors. When that happens, you lose everything: your property, your stuff, your personal protection. Your body—your life—becomes subject to another person's desires, whether good or evil.

I live in Atlanta, which has a large population of refugees. Every one of them has a story to tell of losing everything they had. They left their country because of a well-founded fear of the stronger ones around them. Many of our communities struggle with gangs. The families who live in gang-ruled neighborhoods understand fearing others around them. The bigger guy rules, and the little guys group together to form alliances: "I'll look out for you if you'll look out for me."

Here in Genesis, we read about four strong kings who formed an alliance. They were unstoppable. They defeated every country in the area, reigning over them and dominating their world. Then five little kingdoms—including Sodom and Gomorrah—also formed an alliance. They joined together to fight against the strong alliance of four kingdoms, but they failed. So all their stuff, all their people, got carried off. They had no rights, no power, and no freedom.

Pretend with me for a moment that nothing of the Bible, God's written Word, exists for you—just as it didn't for Abram. There are no Ten Commandments, no "Thou shall love God" and "Thou shall not murder ... steal ... lie," no nation of Israel, no Jerusalem, no temple, and no tabernacle. There is no Moses, no forty years wandering in the desert. None of that exists yet.

All you know are the stories passed down orally through the generations: creation, Adam and Eve, the Tree of Knowledge of Good and Evil, the flood destroying everything except for Noah and his family. All around you, there are a lot of people only looking out for themselves, making alliances with each other.

But you meet a man.

He is a king of a place called Salem.

He is a priest of a God called God Most High (notice, capital letters there).

He brings bread, and he brings wine (an ordinary meal).

He provides nourishment, welcoming you with sustenance.

He lays his hands upon you and blesses you, reminding you that *your victories* are from God Most High.

Melchizedek (Mel-KI-zeh-dek)—what an unusual man to show up in the Valley of Kings along with Abram and the king of Sodom. He is a man who clearly had made an alliance with God Most High. His timing was perfect—after a victory by Abram and before a temptation and bribe from the king of Sodom. Melchizedek was a king—a political leader—yet he was also a priest who represented God Most High to the people around him, bringing bread and wine and blessings.

Now we can look back through the telescope of time and say, "Aha ... this representative of God Most High looks very familiar." He is a glimmer of the Messiah to come. David wrote about him in Psalm 110, this ruler with a mighty, kingly scepter, who sits at the right hand of God. He will be arrayed in holy majesty as a king, and also be "a priest forever, in the order of Melchizedek," as well as judge of the nations on God's day of wrath. That is an amazing passage, and I highly recommend reading it!

Then there is the apostle Paul, writing to the Hebrews, who explained that Jesus is this Messiah, this "high priest forever, in the order of Melchizedek." He has entered the inner sanctuary behind the curtain on our behalf as a holy, blameless, and pure high priest to offer the one perfect sacrifice: Himself (Hebrews 6:19–8:13).

It is so fascinating that this one little appearance by this first priest in Genesis 14 would continue to echo down through the ages to describe God's own Anointed One to come.

But back to the King's Valley and Abram and Melchizedek. After the priest showed up with bread and wine and blessings, we see Abram do something very interesting in response: "Abram gave him a tenth of everything" (Genesis 14:20). This was a "king's share." We don't know exactly who Melchizedek was, but he certainly pointed to a holy priest-king to come. Abram seemed to acknowledge that. Oh, by the way, this place where Melchizedek was king and priest of, Salem, would one day become Jerusalem.[11] Interesting, huh?

Melchizedek had made his alliances—not with men, but with God. Melchizedek is a reminder of what is good and true in the sight of God, King of heaven and earth. Right on the heels of this conversation, we hear a very different conversation, with a very different king—the king of Sodom, who offered his own alliance with our returning hero of the hour, Abram.

The city of Sodom may sound familiar to you, as in "Sodom and Gomorrah." It would soon be a city whose sins were so grievous, and the outcry against it so great, that God would send his angels to investigate. (Just wanted to set the stage here for what's to come.) Well, the king of Sodom offered Abram what he *already possessed*: the wealth, the captured spoils of war that he and his 318 trained men had just risked their necks for! And "Abram the Hebrew" (v. 13—the first time the word "Hebrew" is used in the Bible) said, "No, thanks." He then explained why:

> "I have raised my hand, I have taken an oath, to the LORD—God Most High, Creator of heaven and earth, that I trust Him alone to provide for all my needs. I owe no man anything—I owe Him every-thing. My allegiance is to Him. My allegiance—my binding together—is with God alone. (vv. 22–23, my paraphrase)

What would have happened if Abram had taken the spoils of war from the king of Sodom? That exchange would have formed a relationship between them, an alliance. Unknown to Abram and to the king of Sodom, a little way down the road God would send destruction Sodom's way. The king of Sodom offered an alliance. Abram chose God instead.

It would have been so easy to shake hands with the wrong people. It would have been so easy to load up the riches of others on their camels and go along their merry way. It was the way business was done, and no one would even begin to fault them. But Abram had encountered a king and a priest who reminded him of the power and sovereignty of God. He didn't need what the world had to offer. He already possessed the blessings of God Himself, and that was a much sweeter gift.

I just can't help but dip into the next chapter a little bit. In Genesis 15, God showed up for a little night talk with Abram, and listen to how He introduced Himself: "I am your shield, your very great reward" (v. 1). In other words, "I am the God of protection and provision, and you have chosen wisely."

Where is your allegiance? Who has your devotion, your loyalty? Who have you bound yourself together with? Who do you depend on when the enemy is knocking at the door? If your alliance is with God, if He is your protection and your provision, you have nothing to fear. God Most High, Creator of heaven and earth, will be your shield of protection. God Most High, Creator of heaven and earth, will be your very great reward, and His blessings will go beyond the worth of any small treasures here on this temporary earth.

10
WAITING FOR A CHILD
Read Genesis 15–16

*Humble yourselves, therefore, under God's mighty
hand, that he may lift you up in due time. Cast all
your anxiety on him because he cares for you.*

1 Peter 5:6–7

*I wait for the LORD, my whole being waits, and in
his word I put my hope. I wait for the Lord
more than watchmen wait for the morning, more
than watchmen wait for the morning.*

Psalm 130:5–6 (NIV 2011)

*Out of the depths I cry to you, LORD; Lord, hear
my voice.*

Psalm 130:1–2 (NIV 2011)

Waiting is one of the hardest things we do. Time so often seems to move slowly. Your mind may tend to wander around on its own, conjuring up fear and worst-case scenarios. You want to take control and move things in the right direction, but you are powerless—and all you can do is wait.

In Genesis 15–16 we find the intertwined story of three people, all waiting, thousands and thousands of years ago. All three were waiting for the same thing: the birth of a baby. Abram was waiting for a son. God had promised one, and this old man was only getting older. His wife Sarai was waiting for a son. She had been holding on to hope as she followed Abram all over kingdom come, and she wasn't getting any younger. Hagar was also waiting for the birth of her child, and she was in this situation because she had absolutely no power over anything, including her own body. Let's look at each one as they waited.

First, *Abram* had been on this little road trip with God for quite a while now. God was the one who had initiated this relationship Himself—and here they were. He had promised Abram land, blessing, and descendants. Well, Abram was still waiting. The blessing part seemed to be going along smoothly because he had flocks and a good-sized tribe gathered around him. But there were still a couple of things missing—so he cried out to God with the desires of his heart (from Genesis 15:1–5, my paraphrase):

> "What can You give me? I remain childless! And
>   how can I *know* that I will gain possession of
>   this land You have promised me?"
> The Lord's answer came in word pictures and phys-
>   ical demonstrations:

> "I am your shield" (that is, "I am your protection").
> "I am your great reward" (spiritual and material
>   provision).
> Then God took Abram outside to look up into the
>   nighttime sky: "Count the stars, if indeed you
>   can. These are your descendants—more than
>   you can count."

A few years ago I spent several nights in Bryson Canyon—one of the darkest places left in America.[12] A park ranger there presented a program, and his passion was light pollution. He explained one evening how all our city lights—porch lights, streetlights, lighted buildings, etc.—put so much light into the night sky that we can no longer see the majority of stars in the sky. He had set up telescopes that we could look through to see specific stars, but I was content to simply look up with my naked eye into that very dark sky to see the Milky Way with its hundreds and hundreds of stars. I have read that on a dark night in the Near East, over eight thousand stars are visible.[13] What a mighty promise to an old man waiting for *one* child!

But that nighttime sky with its thousands of stars still wasn't enough reassurance for this old man in his eighties, so the Lord chose to write His promise in blood, as we see in Genesis 15:9–16 (my paraphrase):

> "I will cut a covenant [cut a deal] with you, Abram.
> Bring Me a heifer cow, a goat, a ram—and cut them
> in half. And also bring a dove and a pigeon. Lay out
> the bloody halves opposite each other so there's

a pathway between them. Traditionally you and I would walk that bloody path together, and in doing so, we would be swearing that should we break our agreement with each other, then our penalty would be like these animals to our left and to our right— that we, like the animals, would be cut in half. But, Abram, you cannot keep this oath, this promise, this agreement called a "covenant"—so I will send my blazing torch to pass between the pieces and keep it for both of us.

"And know this: you will have descendants. The child you are waiting for will come. But just as you are now in a thick and dreadful darkness, your descendants also will go through a time of darkness—slavery in a foreign land. It will last four hundred years, and then they will come back to possess this great land."

Abram's descendants would be God's messengers to the world. They would tell of the One True God and how He would send a Messiah, the Anointed One who would rescue the world from death. They would need a podium, a central place to speak from, so God promised them a land where He would bring the world to them. This "promised land" would be a bridge between three continents: Africa, Asia, and Europe. Italy would be to the west, Iran to the east, Turkey to the north, Egypt to the south, bordering the Mediterranean Sea. The world would pass through their land.[14]

Abram responded in faith—belief. Faith is acting in accordance with God's revealed truth and reality. Acting according to God's revealed truth may seem to fly in the face of human logic—which leads us straight to Abram's wife Sarai.

Now, Sarai was also waiting for a child. This was a hard wait—and she probably felt pretty hopeless by now. In that time and culture, to be childless was not only painful; it was also filled with shame. Sarai likely heard questions such as: "What is wrong with you? Why has God not given you children? What sin in your life is keeping Him from blessing you?" Human logic would naturally kick in, and someone might start thinking, "If I want this and it's not happening, then I need to work things out so it *will* happen. *I* need to *fix* things."

With this mindset, Sarai's conversation during the waiting was not with the Lord God but with her very human husband, Abram.

Her solution to "fix things" was to use another human being to do what she could not. Though this seemed to be acceptable in the culture around her at the time, I don't think it was God's suggestion. God really loves to do things that are impossible for people to do. He loves miracles that show His glory and goodness, and that help us understand He alone is God. Sarai's plan was not finding a willing "surrogate" through the internet. No, she had a servant: A woman who had no say in the matter. A woman who had no rights. A woman who did not dare say no to the man and woman who owned her.

Listen to Sarai's part of the conversation from Genesis 16:1–2 (my paraphrase):

"The Lord has kept me from having children" (blame game).

"Perhaps I can build a family through my maidservant" (using another person to get what you want).

So Sarai took her maidservant and *gave* her to her husband (ownership of another human *and* adultery—though this was not officially against the law yet!).

We have trouble picturing this, don't we? Can you imagine how desperate you must be to coerce your husband to have sexual relations with another woman? Obviously, Sarai saw no other possibilities, no other options—and she was willing to sacrifice the most intimate relationship she had. And so it was. What ugliness results when we try to fix things apart from God!

Her maidservant conceived, and suddenly all the relationships changed. Things did not work out the way Sarai imagined, so she went to Abram again (vv. 5–6, my paraphrase):

"You, Abram, are responsible for my suffering!" (There's that blame again!)

"You did what I asked and now look where that has gotten us." (Here we're nodding our heads, *Yep* ...)

"May the Lord judge between you and me!" (Ah, she finally referred to God's power!)

Abram wanted no part of this woman's fury: "She's your problem—do with her whatever you think best."

Sarai was tired of waiting on God—and she took matters into her own hands. Where did this impatience get her? She now had a damaged relationship with her husband. She was receiving contempt from her closest companion within her household. (Can you imagine living with your "friend" who just slept with your husband and is now carrying his baby?) In the process of trying to play God, she just introduced an outsider—a foreigner—into her own family.

Warning! Never underestimate the power of sexual relationships. Our culture would have you believe they are "casual" and "harmless." But there is always a cost.

What a mess. And Sarai lashed out in abuse. She now hated what she thought would bring her happiness. And a baby is on the way. Everybody happy?

Finally, we meet *Hagar*.

Hagar was also waiting. She was pregnant with a child she had been forced to conceive. She was a servant in a foreign land, abused by her mistress, and thus she decided her life was so miserable that she would be better off in the wilderness—alone.

This sounds like a desperate situation to me. Waiting. Alone. In the desert. Pregnant.

The angel of the Lord "found" Hagar there (v. 7). He wasn't just stumbling along and then came across her. He found her because he was looking for her. He knew her by name. He knew her past. He knew her future.

And there came a very sweet, reassuring conversation. First, the angel asked a question to help her get perspective: "Where have you come from, and where are you going?" (v. 8). Then he gave her direction: "Go back ... and submit ..." (v. 9). He followed the command with a promise and a view into the future (vv. 11–12, my paraphrase): "You will have a son, Ishmael—meaning 'God hears'—and his descendants will be too numerous to count. Your son's demeanor will be wild and stubborn and hostile toward all his brothers."

Now all I hear is that she had to go back to her world of slavery, and her son would be a donkey of a man. But she heard something different. Used and abused, she met, there in the desert, a God who cared for her. She met a God who saw her when she felt invisible. "I have now seen the One who sees me" (v. 13). She knew she was not alone in her waiting.

Are you running away from a life you have no control over, like Hagar? Are you suffering under the sin of decisions made by the people around you, and can you see no hope ahead?

Are you taking your life into your own hands, like Sarai, confident that you can fix things on your own? But everything continues to fall apart?

Or are you trying to have faith in God's promises to you, like Abram? You trust—but time is running out, and there seems to be no way your hopes and dreams will ever come true?

Trust Him. Hold on. You are not alone in your waiting. God sees you. God cares for you. The waiting will be worth it.

11

PART 1: GOD IS AN EXTROVERT AND HE IS ALWAYS ON TIME
Read Genesis 17

Many of us have Bibles in which the words of Jesus are printed in red. Well, I wish the publishers of my Bible had done something like that for the spoken words of God. At first, I was thinking I would like blue for all of God's spoken words. Blue is such a pure color—a color that seems eternal and peaceful. But then I remembered that He's the King, so I guess purple would make more sense.

Wouldn't you love to have a Bible with all of God's spoken words in purple? Then we would realize just how often God speaks. We would see how He speaks very clearly to us, and how He spoke to those prophets of old, mere men and women who walked in relationship with Him.

God is not silent, nor is He shy about who He is and the plans He has. In this chapter of twenty-seven verses, He speaks in nineteen of them. All the other verses are simply Abram's response to what God has said in His big purple voice.

"I am," He said, "God Almighty," defining *who* He was—and is (Genesis 17:1).

Next, He said *what* He expected: "Walk before me and be blameless" (v. 1).

Then comes verse after verse of what God's plans were, of what *He was going to do*:

"*I will confirm* my covenant between me and you" (v. 2).

"*I have made you* a father of many nations" (v. 5—and notice the past tense!).

"*I will make* you very fruitful" (v. 6).

"*I will establish* my covenant [our relationship—forever]" (v. 7).

"*I will give* [land] as an everlasting possession to you and your descendants" (v. 8).

"*I will be* their God" (v. 8).

Our God is vocal. He expresses Himself. This must have been so exciting to Abram—and comforting—and, in the true sense of the word, awesome. And intimate.

The other thing we see about God here is that time seems to be important to Him. We often think time is more important to us and that sometimes God is just not working with our timetable. We try to forgive Him, figuring He is busy with other appointments. The first chapter of Genesis almost reads like a day planner: starting with verse 1 ("In the beginning") and verse 5 ("the first day"), it is filled with references to specific amounts of *time*.

There's a lot of controversy over God's version of time. People think that His days can't be our version of days and that His years must have been measured differently. It is impossible to know, but one thing we do know for sure: Abram and Sarai both thought they were way too old to have children. They were desperate enough to pull in another woman to conceive Abram's child (which made quite a mess), and every conversation with God seemed to be about having a child and how time was running out. That conversation was marked by Abram's doubt and God's reassurance.

So yes, let's accept that Abram really might have been ninety-nine years old and his wife Sarai almost ninety, which is totally crazy. But why be God if You can't do totally crazy things to prove that You are God and much bigger than life? If You created life itself, one little tiny baby is not going to be beyond Your capabilities. Maybe the bigger, more difficult issue is building a trusting relationship that will build and grow, generation after generation.

So like the book as a whole, the seventeenth chapter of Genesis is filled with measurements of time: Abram was ninety-nine years old (v. 1), Sarai was nearly ninety (v. 17), she would give birth by this same time next year (v. 21), infant males from then on would be circumcised at eight days old (v. 12), and Abram obeyed God "on that very day" (v. 23). Time is important to God. God's timing is right on time.

I think when we read God's actual words, we start understanding this is no vague and distant God. He isn't simply watching us from some far-off distance, as one popular song goes. No, this God of the Hebrews is specific in declaring in no uncertain terms who He is and what He expects. He has plans, He makes promises, and He has specific times in mind. I like that. The really cool thing is we now have a few thousand years on our side so we can look back, just as Abram looked forward, and say, "God was right! He could do and then did all those things He said He would. Well, I'll be. He might just know what He is doing."

So where does this belong in my life? Can I trust God's words and His promises? Should I try to hold Him to my schedule, or should I trust His timing? Most importantly, is there anything impossible for God Almighty?

12
PART 2: AN INTIMATE RELATIONSHIP WITH THE KING
Read Genesis 17

In our culture today the most prevalent form of covenant we have is marriage. In many ways it defines us. Some of us are in a marriage covenant. Some of us were in a marriage covenant that was broken for one reason or another. Some of us are waiting to see if we will enter a marriage covenant in the future. A few have decided their life is better lived by not entering into a marriage covenant. This marriage covenant, then, is an important agreement between people that affects how they live their lives.

As we get into part 2 of our look at Genesis 17, Abram and God have been kind of "dating"—I guess you could really say they are "engaged" at this point in terms of a covenantal relationship akin to marriage. God has made His intentions clear to Abram:

> "This is how I feel about you: I am crazy about you
> and want you to spend your life with Me!"

"This is how I plan to provide for you: I want to give you a home—land to call your own."

"I want to give you children: I am going to give you descendants that outnumber the stars in the sky!"

"I want to be your God alone: I want an exclusive relationship with you. I am jealous of your love and cannot stand the thought of you loving any other gods."

God desired an intimate relationship with Abram. The "date was set," and in many ways, this was their wedding day. It was a pretty interesting event.

Three very important elements were involved in the ceremony, much like they are in weddings now:

1. Names were changed. This established the identity of the participants of the covenant. Think of it as going from "Miss" to "Mrs." and changing your maiden name to your married name.

2. Promises were made. This stated the "terms of the covenant." Think of it as the wedding vows.

3. Wedding rings were exchanged—but it was a one-ring ceremony. This was the outward sign of the covenant. Think of how a ring signifies "I belong exclusively to you and this relationship."

Let's first talk more about this name-changing business. Our names are important. They are personal to us. Changing our names only happens in intimate relationships—often as a form of submission (yes, that word!) to and trust in another person's love and care for us.

My mother certainly had a lot of names in her time—and each name change came out of a relationship. Her parents named her Mary Pauline Cunningham. Her four older brothers nicknamed her (to her torment) Lorraine-razoo-pecaner-too. Her girlfriends in nurses training started calling her Polly (which stuck for the rest of her life). When she married her first husband, she became Mrs. Joe Farber. After his death, when she married her second husband, she went from Polly Cunningham Farber to Mrs. Joe Tanner. My point is that our names tell a story of our intimate relationships.

God came to Abram and called Himself by a new name: El Shaddai in Hebrew—God Almighty in English (v. 1). The meaning is "Invincible Power" or "God, the Mountain One." This name for God appears forty-eight times in the Bible—especially in the book of Job—and it has great and powerful imagery associated with it.[15] God the Mountain One. Think of all the hills surrounding Jerusalem—one of them is Mount Zion. Think of Mount Sinai, where God met with Moses on the mountaintop. Think of David's song:

> I lift up my eyes to the hills—
> where does my help come from?
> My help comes from the LORD,
> the Maker of heaven and earth. (Psalm 121:1)

God gave a new name for Himself in this relationship with Abram: "I am Invincible Power. I am Rock-Solid Mountain." He also gave Abram a new name (v. 5): changing it from Abram, meaning "high or exalted father" (ironic for a man with no children most of his life, eh?) to Abraham, meaning father of a

multitude (well, again, it just got even more awkward, right?).
God gave Sarai a new name also (v. 15): from Sarai, meaning "my princess" (perhaps a reference to her noble descent)
to Sarah, meaning "royal princess" (from whom kings would
come). Then, sweetest of all, God gives the promised child of
the covenant a name (v. 19): Isaac, meaning "he laughs"!

Have you ever been so surprised by something that you
laugh out loud without thinking? Can you picture it? This old
man, wrinkled and gray, a leader of a growing tribe, lying facedown in the dirt, dust covering his face, trying to be respectful to God Almighty, who is talking to him about incredibly
important things. Yet there he is, shaking with laughter at
the thought of having a son at his age (v. 17). Giggling, you
might say. What a great relationship! I'm with Abraham. I
think God has a great sense of humor—He surprises me all
the time!

When Jeff and I planned to get married, we were not attending church, nor was our relationship with God very active at
that time. We had both put God on a shelf for the time being.
But I knew two things concerning our wedding ceremony: I
wanted to be married by a "real preacher" in a religious ceremony (not a justice of the peace), and I wanted the "till death
do us part" in the wedding vows.

Well, God goes way beyond "till death do us part." His
relationships are so important to Him that they go on and on
without end. They are everlasting from generation to generation. Let's take a look at that covenantal vow. God initiated it
(15:18), He confirmed it (17:2), and He established it (v. 7). He
was very clear: "I am committed to you and I require you to
be committed to Me—because I desire an everlasting, covenant

relationship with you." This is no temporary, "We'll see how things work out" kind of thing.

"You will be Mine, and I will be your God." It is an intimate, exclusive, marriage vow. Interestingly there is conversation within the ceremony—there is the "But what about Ishmael?" question (v. 18). It was a question that Abraham needed to ask. "What do we do about the results of me going off on my own? What about Ishmael, the son of my mistrust of You? Can't we change Your plan?" In verses 20–21, God answered, "I have heard you. I will bless him. I will make him fruitful. I will make him into a great nation. But My plan doesn't change. It is your son Isaac, the son I have promised, who will carry the blessings of My covenant with you."

Here we see the wonder of God. Even when we turn our backs and go off with our own agenda, thinking we can create our own destiny apart from God, He doesn't turn away from us. "Yes, I hear you," He says. "I will turn your wrong into My right. But I am God, and I have a plan that is bigger than you." It is the continuing story of God's grace. And so it would be Isaac who would have descendants—including Jacob (Israel), David, Jesus—that would fulfill these marriage promises.

Now for the ring, please. It is the outward sign of the covenant. The "ring" that God gave to Abraham and all within his household was the rite of circumcision for males. We continue this practice in our culture for medical and hygienic reasons, but for Abraham, it was to be a sign of trust and obedience. It symbolized an oath: "I cut off my foreskin to be a constant reminder that I never want to be 'cut off' from You, O Lord."

On that very day, Abraham and all the males in his household underwent circumcision. Going forward, every eight-day-old male infant would be permanently marked by this rite of circumcision, coming under this covenant with God. The resulting ring of flesh was a constant reminder—"I belong to God." It was an important day.

I think of the thin gold ring I have in my jewelry box. Engraved inside that circle of gold, I can read *JAT+PCF 3-12-55*—the initials of my parents and the date of their wedding, permanently joined together, cut into the gold of that band as an oath of their exclusive, permanent relationship.

God still desires an everlasting covenantal relationship with us. He pursues us with an everlasting love. When we say yes, He changes our name. He names us after His Son, the Christ, and from that time on, we each become known as a Christian. He makes a promise to us: "Whoever believes in [the Christ] shall not perish but have everlasting life" (John 3:16). He marks us with His sign, the symbol of His promise to us: His Spirit comes to live within us. And His Spirit within us will become as obvious as a ring on our finger. His Spirit will be a constant reminder to us and an outward marking to others that we are in an exclusive, permanent relationship with our King—the one true God.

Have you ever realized that God pursues you? How do the relationships you have had with others affect how you view your relationship with God? How would your life change if you entered into an exclusive, intimate relationship with Almighty God? He is waiting for your answer.

13
GOD SPEAKS
Read Genesis 18

The Lord came to Abraham
in the form of three men;
standing nearby,
they waited.
The Lord and two angels
in the form of flesh and blood
able to eat
able to drink
able to rest and wait and talk.
The Lord appearing as three.
We understand this—easily—
because we also know
of a God of one
appearing as three
Father, Holy Spirit, Son.
Three appearing as One.
One appearing as three.
Abraham is no longer

lying in the dust in awe and reverence.

He is very busy instead.

He hurries to meet them, bowing low.

He offers them the hospitality of foot-washing
and refreshment.

He hurries to Sarah's tent, "Make bread and lots of it!"

He hurries to select the choicest calf from the herd
and hurries the servant to prepare it.

Serving the Lord,

three in one,

he waits close by

to respond to their needs.

And we begin to understand why

the Lord, in the form of three,

is there.

They are there for Sarah with the good news of life.

They are there for Sodom and Gomorrah with the
terrifying news of death.

They are there for Abraham to trade confidences.

In the telling of this story in Genesis 18, we see the Lord in ways we have never seen Him. He comes to Abraham in bodily form: human flesh and blood. Did Abraham recognize Him in the beginning? It's hard to say. But Abraham certainly knew who He was before He left: the Lord went from "lord" with a little *l* in verse 3 to "Lord" with a big *L* in verse 27.

This Lord with the big *L* revealed a great deal about Himself: His plans for the future as well as His capabilities to judge right from wrong, righteous from wicked. In that role of Judge, He also had—and has—the ability to punish with death or offer mercy and life. We also see the Lord with the big *L* in relationship with His creation. He knew their thoughts (Sarah), He heard their cries (Sodom and Gomorrah), and He spoke with them in confidence (Abraham).

Let's get to know this flesh-and-blood Lord of Abraham, and hear the Lord tell of something good He was going to do.

Likewise, a few years ago I had this experience of hearing God tell me something He was going to do, and I was nowhere near as polite or complacent as Sarah. No little titter of amused laughter from me. I flat out said, "No, no, no. I do not want to do this, Lord!"

God had decided—and I am not sure why—that He was going to have an extremely handsome German man attend Good Friday worship services in Atlanta that week.

With me.

At first, when I was praying one evening and I distinctly heard the voice of God speaking to me (and I have to say this is definitely *not* something I normally experience!), it seemed like a thing I could possibly handle—though I didn't want to. I am a director and I was praying for the process and for the film crew who would be working with me on a commercial spot we were shooting up at Lake Lanier that Friday. And I heard God speak: "Invite the people you are working with to the Good Friday evening service at your church."

I really try to keep work and God separate. Not because of some work ethic, but because I am a chicken, and I know very well that film and God don't usually walk hand in hand—and I am extremely dependent on what other people think of me for my next job. I kind of try to keep my faith walk on the down-low. Like I said, chicken. But God loves to pull these kinds of stunts with me, so I wasn't too surprised. Before I could protest too much, God completed His sentence: "And Michael is going to accept."

We had flown Michael over from Germany (because Lord knows there are no handsome brunet men here in America). I didn't know the guy, except that he was rather intimidating in all his German beauty, and he winked whenever you looked at him—and he had a reputation for lounging around without his shirt or much else on (picture Abercrombie & Fitch here).

So I did, and he did, and then I knew God was on His way to doing something bigger than me. There was absolutely no way on a Friday afternoon that we could have made it from sailboat and sunscreen through five o'clock Friday I-85 traffic all the way to the heart of Buckhead—with someone who didn't even normally go to my church holding seats for us, as Michael, freshly showered at his hotel that just "happened" to be next door to the church, slipped into the row, stood next to me, and winked. God had plans.

I still don't know exactly what those plans were—and I probably never will. But God wanted Michael there that evening. And he was. He came back again, flying in from Germany, to smile and ice skate and make the clothes look good as he held a beautiful model's hand. And to spend the weekend with my family, talking late into the night by the bonfire in our backyard, sleeping in the guestroom, attending church with us on Sunday, and holding hands with us for every blessing over every meal.

I tell you all of this because I understand Sarah laughing when God told her His plans. I understand her laughing when God asked for her by name and then told her she would have a son by that time the next year. Because, yes, sometimes in our minds and hearts, things seem too big, too hard, too wonderful to believe—and we just laugh to ourselves and say, "No way!" And we need to hear God say, "Yes, I know what you are thinking: *This is too hard, too impossible.'* And you are right: it is. It really is ... for you—but not for Me."

If our confidence is in ourselves, some things in our lives will be too hard. If our confidence is in the Lord, nothing is too hard.

Then we get to the problem of Sodom and Gomorrah. For four years I worked in retail with staffs made up of gay men. Eight hours a day, five days a week, I spent lots of time in conversation with them, and I know way more than I ever wanted to know about the sexual practices and thoughts of those particular men. I will not go into detail. But though I was close to many of them, I do not doubt for a second the scene you can read about in Genesis 19:4–5—of all the men, from every part of the city of Sodom, surrounding the house and threatening to break down the door to have sex with the two handsome male travelers inside (who were actually angels).

I left that job in part because I could not continue to listen day after day as some of the guys I worked with ogled strangers—everyday businessmen—as they walked by. I know the same thing can happen with heterosexual men or women, looking at people as potential sexual conquests. But one day I reached a turning point. Their words were so disturbing and offensive to my ears and to my soul that I decided I could stand it no longer.

The Lord told Abraham, "I can stand it no longer. The outcry against these people in Sodom and Gomorrah is so great and their sins so grievous that I must destroy them" (18:20–21).

Here we see a powerful picture of God, as He stood there in human form, talking with Abraham. His angels were already on their way to investigate the cry for justice, and it became evident that this Lord is Judge of all the earth. He hears the cry of those who call out for justice. He does not treat the wicked and the innocent the same. His judgment is fair and right. He will punish the wicked and spare the righteous. He has ears that hear and eyes that see, and He acts as Judge of the earth.

We all have seen those who are wicked slip through the cracks and continue to hurt and harm anyone in their path. We have also seen situations where a wrong or harsh judgment can ruin someone's life forever. Abraham showed us a God we can trust for righteous judgment—and all we have to do is cry out. He hears us.

We see Abraham, no longer lying in the dust, but standing, pleading with Almighty God, Judge of all the earth, for mercy. What gave him such boldness? It came because God Himself decided to confide in Abraham. God said out loud, "Shall I hide from Abraham what I am about to do?" And He decided, "No, I will confide in him—because I have chosen him. I have chosen him as a friend, as a confidante" (vv. 17–19, my paraphrase).

This idea of God confiding in Abraham is amazing! James, the half brother of Jesus, was so amazed by it that he wrote about it in his book, saying, "Abraham ... was called God's friend" (James 2:23). In Isaiah 41:8 we hear God call Abraham "my friend." Abraham was *friends* with God!

What is a friend? Not an acquaintance, or a work associate, or the neighbor next door that you chat with—but a "deep heart, share anything, come into your house without knocking" kind of friend. We have very few of those. It is someone you confide in. There's a level of trust and shared expectations. In this small story, God confided in Abraham, and Abraham confided in the Lord: "I trust You. I know who You are. This is where I will boldly place my confidence."

Jesus told His disciples, "I call you friends, and I share with you what My Father has shared with Me. You did not choose Me, but I chose you" (John 15:15–16, my paraphrase). You only confide in someone if you have established trust in that person or that relationship.

I want to have confidence in God. I want to be able to confide in Him. And wouldn't it be wonderful to think that God could confide in me? That God could trust me when He wants to use my mouth or my hands or my feet or my house or my guest room?

A few years back I attended a business convention aboard a cruise ship. I would get up early in the morning while it was still dark and head up to the top level of the ship to watch the sun rise as I walked the jogging track. The first morning I almost tripped over a young worker as he scrubbed the stairs leading to the top deck. The next morning I found him in the same place. Southern girl that I am, I initiated pleasantries as I passed him the second time: "Oh, it is so cloudy today. I wonder if it is going to rain?" He said, "Oh no, it will clear!" His accent sounded heavy, perhaps Eastern European. He looked pale and a bit fragile to be out there in the darkness of morning, scrubbing stairs.

My third and last morning, I went up by a different staircase and started my walk. I felt curious, though, and soon peeked over the rail to look down the other staircase I'd used the previous two days. There he was, scrubbing those stairs.

My heart started beating fast. I have found that to be the way the Holy Spirit leads me sometimes: a quickened heartbeat, a thought that is urgent and strong and becomes more and more insistent. There is no ignoring it.

I was in gym shorts and a T-shirt, with only my room key and a $20 bill that I'd stuck into my pocket three days before in case I needed it. God confided in me: "That young man needs to know I am with him." My response, "Lord, can't I just do my walk?" My heart started beating faster, my hands shook, and then He gave me the words He wanted me to say. I took one more lap but became frantic that the young man might leave before I delivered my message.

As I descended the stairs, the sun was rising behind him and the wind was blowing with a slight morning chill. He stopped scrubbing as I stood on his step and held out the money to him. "This is for you," I said.

He looked at the money and then at me—fearfully. "No, it is too much!"

I looked into his eyes and delivered my message: "God is with you, and Jesus knows who you are."

With that, he accepted the gift.

God calls us out of our comfort zone when He confides in us—because He cares about us and the people around us. And He wants us to confide in Him. Who are you worried about? Who are you concerned about? I am willing to bet that God is concerned about them too. Abraham was worried about his nephew Lot and his family. God sent angels to literally pull them by the hand out of harm's way.

Do you think God is aware of what is going on in our world? Do you trust God to judge? Do you think He hears our cries for justice and defends those who cannot defend themselves? Can you trust God when He asks you to do something that makes you feel awkward or ridiculous? Do you believe you could be God's friend?

You can confide in the Lord with the capital *L*. He is the God of justice. He tells us to come to Him in boldness and to call out for those who need His justice, to call out for those who need His salvation—over and over again. He will hear us.

14
RELUCTANT TO BE RESCUED
Read Genesis 19

Oh, to sit in the gates of the city—
to be known and respected,
connected,
with the people who come and go around you.
"She is wise," they say. "Let's ask her advice."
Successful in business, responsible,
    a person of her word.
The biggest house on the hill,
the handsome husband,
children well mannered,
with bows in their hair.
His son is captain of the soccer team,
his daughter is on the dean's list,
he's a mover and a shaker
    and his company was just named
    one of the most successful in the city.

We are attracted to what sparkles
    in the eyes of others.
We are drawn to accolades
    and the praise of our peers.
We want to be liked, well thought of,
    by our neighbors.
We want to be voted "Most Popular"
    or "Most Likely to Succeed"
    by our fellow students.
Even if we deny it, it sneaks around,
    underneath our skin, peeking out to surprise us
    at the most unexpected times.
It is hard to be content to sit
    at the entrance of our tent;
we would rather be sitting in the gates of the city.
There is a word that describes it,
    this deep, deep feeling.
It's a word we don't use much anymore:
"Longing."

There's not much said about Lot's wife except
    that she turned into a pillar of salt.
Was she a good mother? A loving wife?
A gracious neighbor or a loving friend?
We don't know.
There is one thing we do know about her:
"She looked back with longing."
This wasn't a casual backward glance
    to say goodbye. This was a "How can I live
    without what I am leaving?" kind of longing.

Longing for something we do not have
    blinds us to what we do have.
It blurs our vision in a far-sighted kind of way.
We can't see what we have in our hands today,
because we are longing
    for what we could have tomorrow.
Or what could have been—but is not—
    out there in the distance.

What drew nephew Lot into the city?
Longing.
What caused him to sit in the mud with evil?
Longing.
What caused him to disregard the spiritual
and physical protection of his daughters?
Longing.
Why did he return to Sodom
after Abraham rescued him from captivity?
Longing.

What do we long for that holds us
    captive and blind?
Lot was captive in his own home
as all the men of the city, young and old,
threatened him harm,
    preparing to break the door in.
Angels intervened to make his enemies blind,
to buy a little time to reason with him—
and still, he stayed,
    paralyzed with longing.

This is a story of rescue and rejection.
It is completely unreasonable, irrational.
Why would God choose to rescue
    Lot and his family?
And why would Lot reject being rescued?
Why was he unable to see the danger at hand?
It was because he was longing for prestige among
    his enemies.
Reluctant to be rescued,
Lot, his wife, his daughters, his future sons-in-law—
even the town of Sodom itself
rejected the Mercy of God.
"We don't need to be saved. We're fine.
We're busy longing for this other thing."

As the story of Genesis 19 begins, we find Lot sitting in the gateway of Sodom: the gateway of Sin City. He had not only made his home there; he also had become one of its leaders. Yet he was a vine producing no flower, no fruit. He had no sphere of influence. He was affecting no one's life for good. Where were his "318 trained men born in his household" prepared to rescue the captives? (Remember Abraham a few years back when he came to Lot's rescue? See Genesis 14:11–16.)

Living a compromised life has little reward.

Choosing to live outside God's Promised Land holds little promise. Instead, the sin of the culture makes you numb.

And you slowly become the people you hang out with.

Their thoughts resonate in your head.

Their values press into yours.

You become Silly Putty in their hands, all without realizing it. Because of your longing.

So here we have Lot—with sin literally banging on his door. God intervened, riding in on His white horse, sending down His angels of protection and destruction. (Isn't it interesting how they can be both?) They *reached out* and *pulled* Lot back in and *shut* the door, then *struck* the enemy with blindness. Wow! What a God of action and power!

We shortchange God and His mighty power all day long. I know I do. I completely think God is too small or too busy to deal with my fears and my enemies at the door.

But that is not what we see here:

> He sends angels in human form,
> to visit and evaluate,
> to warn of coming destruction,
> to reach out and physically pull Lot to safety,
> to offer protection to anyone
>   in Lot's sphere of influence, saying,
> "God not only cares about rescuing you—
> He also desires to rescue others—
> especially those people you care about—
> those people He has placed in your life."

In the end, with the coming of dawn, as Lot still hesitated with longing, God's angels *physically reached out* and "grasped his hand and the hands of his wife and of his two daughters" and *physically led* them away from danger (19:16).

Because God is merciful. Because God rescues.

One of the angels warned them, "Flee for your lives! Don't look back with longing! Run and don't stop or you will be swept away!"

It is then that we see the longing of Lot's heart. Unlike Abraham, who negotiated with God for mercy for others—"Spare their lives, O Lord with the capital *L*, O God of justice, Judge of the earth!"—Lot negotiated for something very different. Lot negotiated for the city gates of a smaller city. Lot was still longing for the things and influence possible in the culture around him.

"I don't need to be rescued," he insisted. "Well, maybe a little bit—but if I have to leave this big, evil city, let me go instead to this little one."

Lot still rejected the actuality of being rescued. *I can't flee or I'll die,* he thought, *because underneath it all, I long for the sin found in the city. I long for the life I am familiar with, the life I am comfortable with.*

The sun was high. It had risen, and God's destruction rained down, destroying evil and burning the land with fire and brimstone. Standing far off, in the place where he had stood with the Lord, Abraham saw the smoke of judgment and destruction, knowing that the God of judgment was also the God of rescue and mercy.

> There will be Another
> who will tell of coming destruction
> of fire to rain from the sky
> with the coming of "the day."
> He will be a descendant from Abraham,
> who will preach a message of rescue:

"The Spirit of the Lord is on *Me*,
because He has anointed *Me*
to preach good news to the poor.
He has sent *Me* to proclaim
    freedom for the prisoners
and recovery of sight for the blind
(rescue offered to both sides of the door!)
to release the oppressed
to proclaim the year of the Lord's favor."[16]

God is on a mission of rescue
and He sent his very own Son in flesh and blood
    to reach out,
to take our hand,
and physically pull us into safety
    and out of danger.
But we resist, we refuse, we reject.
Jesus knew our longings ...
our longings for the things that harm us.
He knew of our blindness,
and our comfort with our sin and bondage.
"He who listens to you listens to Me;
he who rejects you rejects Me;
but he who rejects Me
rejects Him who sent Me."[17]

God offers His hand in rescue.

There is a sad and repulsive ending to the story of Lot and his longings. Read it for yourself.

His wife looked back with longing,
and his daughters looked forward with longing,
for children they thought they couldn't have.
And night has fallen again.
Rape is nothing new
and unfortunately, incest is an old, old story.
But it is still surprising when it is women
    who are the ones plotting the evil.
If you lean into evil long enough,
    it has an effect on you—
and that effect multiplies from a baby to a nation.

Lot's two daughters, the older and the younger, could see no solution to their longings for children, other than the unthinkable. Their own father, Lot, had offered them to the madmen on the other side of the door to be raped as substitutes—and now they chose to rape their own father as a substitute for a proper husband and honorable father for their children. Their babies would be named Moab and Ben-Ammi and would become the nations of the Moabites and the Ammonites—bitter enemies of Abraham's descendants.

"I am here to rescue you," God says.
We all need to be rescued.
We, like Lot and his wife and his daughters,
and even those evil men, blind,
    on the other side of the door,
all need to be rescued.

What does this story tell us about ourselves? What are we longing for that separates us from God? What holds us captive? Are there people God has placed in our lives that He longs to rescue? Are we longing to sit in the city gates or are we holding tightly to the hand of God as He leads us to unknown lands? Morning is coming and the sun will be rising soon.

And it is not the end of the story:

> The One sent to rescue us
> warns us,
> "For the Son of Man is going to come
> in His Father's glory with His angels
>   (sound familiar?)
> and then He will reward
> each person
> according to what he has done."[18]

> And there it is:
> We have a choice how we respond to God's rescue.
> We can reject God's hand,   .
> in the way of Lot ...
> or we can receive God's mercy
>   and share in His reward,
> in the way of Abraham.
> What do you choose?

15
FEARLESS
Read Genesis 20–21

Fear. It is such a powerful emotion. It can keep us safe from harm. The hairs stand up on our arms and blood surges through our veins, powering up the courage to fight with all our might or triggering the response to run for our lives.

Fear of the wrong things, though, can do the opposite. Fear that paralyzes us can endanger our lives. We choose to not move forward. We choose to stay where we are and play it safe. We hide truths, deny danger, and take the easiest way out. We click the locks closed on our doors and pull a blanket over our heads.

Most of us have known that kind of unreasonable, paralyzing fear in our lives. I have. For years I struggled with panic attacks. Mine were triggered when I was pregnant with my second child. Though I had flown for years with no problems, while waiting on the runway moving forward for takeoff, my eyes suddenly filled with tears, and out of nowhere, I became terrified of flying. My heart raced and my hands shook as I stared out the window, trying to keep the plane aloft with my willpower alone. It was horrible—especially since I flew often for work. If I had an upcoming trip, my heart would start beating fast just hearing a plane fly low overhead.

I also became terrified of driving over bridges that crossed water. Late one afternoon, during a winter rain traveling from my mother's house in Greenville back home to Atlanta, I vowed to God if He would get me safely across that bridge over Lake Hartwell, I would pull over and check myself into a hotel for the night at the next exit. And I did. Because I could not stop the terrible fear of what I would do if my car, with two sleeping children strapped into car seats in the backseat, plunged off the bridge and into the icy water.

Fear. It can be a horrible demon to deal with.

God has something to say about fear: "Do not. Do not fear. Do not fear for I am with you. My rod and My staff will bring you comfort." Most of us are familiar with the wonderful words of that last phrase from the Twenty-Third Psalm. The shepherd David wrote that song about God being a Shepherd to His people. David knew about being a good shepherd. It was his responsibility as the youngest boy in his family to spend his days and nights in the open field, keeping watch over the family's sheep. The two tools he always had with him were his rod and his staff.

Sheep, apparently, are not smart animals. Left on their own, they would quickly die. They need a shepherd to take care of the basics: finding them green grass to fill their bellies and water to quench their thirst. They wander off on their own and fall into ravines or get caught up in brambles. They stand there powerless and bleat. The good shepherd, keeping careful watch over his sheep, notices when one of them is missing. He leaves the flock to look for the one who has gone astray. When he finds it helpless and in trouble, he reaches out the hook of his staff to encircle its neck and pull it out of harm's way and into his loving arms of safety. Predators are quick to attack a lone sheep, but a heavy rod can reach into the fray of snarling wolves and fight them off, safely rescuing the terrified, frozen-with-fear lamb.

David knew that under the good shepherd's watchful eye, the fearful lamb had little to fear. David also knew that whatever situation he encountered, his watchful Shepherd, the Lord God, was watching over him. "Do not fear."

In Genesis 20–21 we find stories of people paralyzed by fear. Fear that made them hide and lie and be cruel to others and give up in despair. For them God was "a long ways off" and they were certain they had been abandoned. No good shepherd was going to show up with his rod and his staff.

We just watched God rain down burning sulfur in judgment on the people of Sodom and Gomorrah. Lot didn't quite seem to notice that God had placed angels right by his side to physically pull him out of those doomed places. Good grief, Lot—what does it take? You had two angels telling you what to do and leading you by the hand. But no, it was too much for you and you planted yourself, shaking in your boots, in a little town called Zoar, which means "small." But small Zoar was not small enough for you, and the next thing we hear, while Abraham was on a high place looking out over a plain, you had packed your two daughters up, infused them with fear, and moved them into something even smaller: a cave.

This is a pretty good picture of what fear does to us. God came to rescue Lot, and he chose the dark, solitary life of a cave instead. God knows we need fellowship, we need room to spread out, and we need far horizons to set our sights on. Fear shuts everything down. It looks for dark places to hide. The story continues, going from bad to worse. From Lot and his two daughters, we have the beginning of the Moabites and the Ammonites: two tribes that will be unbelievers in the Good Shepherd and will be adversaries of God's people.

Now we catch up with Abraham: our Abraham who has been traveling along this road with God for a while now. Lo and behold, old habits are hard to break, and we see Abraham acting out of fear again instead of trusting God for His provision and protection. We watch, aghast, as he lies, deceives, and stumbles on the eve of God fulfilling his long-awaited promise—as he again passes his wife Sarah off as his sister (20:1–2).

"Oh, she's just my sister. No need to kill me to get her. You just go ahead and take her for your harem. I'll be over here minding my own business."

What? Abraham! Why do you do this? This little lie to protect yourself is so weird and so steeped in fear. And we wives are saying, "Sarah, are you really going to go along with this?" It makes me wonder what living in a harem was like. Maybe a little like going to the spa after hiking around in the dusty desert for years. A little fellowship with other women, a hot bath, pretty clothes, peeled grapes, and a pedicure. Okay, maybe that wasn't such a bad deal for Sarah.

But God wasn't too happy about it (vv. 3–7). He showed up in Abimelech's dreams and basically said, "Hey, Abimelech! You are as good as dead!"

Boy, don't you know that got his attention.

"This woman you have brought into your home is a married woman. And because this doesn't sit well with Me—Almighty God—I have closed the womb of every woman in your household ... and given you some problems in your manhood as well. Return her to her husband, who, by the way, is a prophet for Me. He will pray for you and all your women here to be healed, and you can go along on your merry way." Boy, God went to some extreme measures to make sure Sarah didn't become pregnant while in Abimelech's house!

So early the next morning, Abimelech gathered all his men and told them what was going on. We read, "They were very much afraid" (v. 8). Their fear didn't lead them to a dark cave though. It prompted them to bring everything that had been hidden in darkness out into the light (vv. 9–16). "Abraham, what is up with you?" Abimelech asked. "We never intended to harm you! Why did you put us in danger with you and your God? You shouldn't have done this. Take your wife. No harm, no foul. Take these gifts as a measure of our apologies. Live in our land wherever you please." They were humbled in the face of fear of the Lord and thus brought everything out into the light, where forgiveness could happen and relationships could be restored.

Have you ever been put in a dangerous situation by the lies and deceptions of another? What was your reaction? Anger, understandably. Fear of consequences you could face because of another's careless actions? We see here such a powerful and effective reaction to this situation: an honest confrontation in the light, wrapped up in humility and forgiveness. Abimelech, confronted by God in a dream, certainly stood taller than

Abraham, hiding in a lie. I think his actions reflect a healthy fear of God—even though Abraham was accusing him of the opposite.

Good for you, Abimelech.

Abraham took his wife and they went on their way. Suddenly, finally, without much fanfare, the long-awaited son of Abraham and Sarah was born. Abraham was an old, old man. Over a hundred years old. Sarah was not too far behind at ninety. "Impossible!," we may say. Well, exactly. God wants us to understand clearly that what is impossible with man is a walk in the park for Him. Hence, the "Do not fear."

Why the long wait? Sarah surely wondered.

Some things we will never understand, but maybe it took these many years for Abraham to trust God completely. Abraham had to trust God enough to give him a son so that he could trust God when He would ask Abraham to give him up. All we know right now is that this long-awaited son was given a beautiful name: Isaac, meaning "laughter." We remember Abraham lying in the dust, laughing, listening to God's promises. We see Sarah hidden behind the tent a year ago, laughing out loud when God showed up for lunch with the promise of a coming son. We are sure, now, as this baby boy was wrapped in the wrinkled arms of Sarah, that her tent was filled with laughter. Isaac was a fine name for the long-awaited child. His birth brought great joy to a woman who had continued to hold on to a thin thread of hope when things seemed hopeless.

They threw a party and invited everyone to celebrate. But there he was, the reminder of Sarah's impatience with God: Ishmael. Fear welled up in Sarah.

What if that firstborn child of Abraham, born of a slave, became more important to Abraham than her own son, born of laughter? What if God forgot His promise that her son, Isaac, would be the son of the covenant? What if, what if, what if ...?

Her fears haunted her, dancing around in her brain, encircling her heart. Sarah feared for her son's future, so the easiest solution was to get rid of the first son and his slave mother—banish them to the desert where the sun and sand should take care of them quickly enough (21:8–10).

God, oddly enough, allowed it. And Abraham did it. He handed them a canteen of water and a picnic lunch, then sent them on their way (vv. 11–14). Destination: certain death.

Doesn't this make us pause and say, "Wait, wait, wait! God said what? Did He seriously say, 'Don't worry about it. Send them on their way, because, yes, what Sarah says is right: Isaac is the one and only son of the blessing'?"

Don't we want to be "fixers" in the tent with them, saying, "Hold on, God and Abraham—let's not be so hasty about this. Can't we just set up a nice little house for them on the other side of town? Isn't there a better solution than banishing them to death in the desert?"

Yet we see something interesting in Abraham here (other than his apparent heartlessness): Abraham trusted God. He was fearful for the future of Hagar and Ishmael, but he still trusted God when He essentially said, "I've got this, Abraham." So Abraham led his firstborn son and the boy's mother out into the desert.

Then we hear Hagar's story (vv. 14–21). How many times would she eventually tell this miraculous story to others? Alone in the desert of Beersheba, water gone, food gone, sun high in

the sky and scorching the ground, she placed her son in the little shade she could find and then walked away—just far enough
to deafen her to the cries she couldn't bear to hear as he died.
With fear shaking Hagar to her soul while awaiting death, she
cried out to God. She could not bear to hear her son's cries, but
God could—and did. He alone was there to rescue them.

"Do not be afraid," He said to her (v. 17). There is that command again—the one that defeats fear. "I am here with you,"
God told her (vv. 17–18, my paraphrase). "I see you. I hear you.
I will provide for you. I will open your eyes. Here is water. Here
is life. Take your son by the hand and guide him—because as I
promised Abraham, I will make him into a great nation."

God was with the boy as he grew to be a young man and
a mighty nation, living in the desert of Paran (vv. 20–21). He
and his descendants would not wander too far from the tents
of their father, Abraham. God, ever the Good Shepherd, would
continue His watch over His sheep.

There is one more story in this passage; it seems odd and
quite honestly uninteresting. It is the story of a well at Beersheba. Abraham was still a nomad in a foreign land. He was
a stranger with no land of his own, living in the land of the
Philistines. Abimelech, the king of Gerar, was a great ruler of
the Philistines, mighty and powerful. Why would he care anything about this roaming nomad Abraham? Why would it be
important to him to be on good terms with this unimportant
guy? Why bother?

Abimelech showed up to talk with Abraham, along with the
commander of his fighting men by his side—so it seemed like a
show of force. Yet the king's words were a negotiation of peace.
Could it be that this mighty man was a bit afraid of Abraham

and his God? "Hey," Abimelech said to Abraham, "I'm notic-ing your God is making you successful in everything you do. I want you to promise me that you and I will be friends—and our children and their children will be friends, generation after generation. I don't want any trouble with you. I want to live in peace with you" (vv. 22–23, my paraphrase).

Clearly, Abimelech had seen something different about Abraham—and we have this unusual testimony of God's faith-fulness through the eyes of a pagan king. Abimelech approached Abraham as an equal and asked for a covenant between the two of them and their descendants. This was monumental! Look at what he was saying: Abimelech was confident that Abraham would have descendants that would settle permanently in that land. He saw God fulfilling His promises to Abraham. Perhaps because of that, Abimelech desired a covenant of peace. It was a *promise of peace*, not a threat of fear.

Living in a foreign land? No worries because God will always give the same command: "Do not fear."

Then there is the little issue of the well. In the desert having a well is crucial. In those times if you had water in the desert, you had permanent and legal rights to the land. If the well belonged to Abimelech, then it was his land. If the well belonged to Abra-ham, then that changed things. Interestingly we see Abimelech accepting Abraham's "payment" of seven lambs. Abraham did something else that was significant: he planted a tamarisk tree there in Beersheba. A tamarisk tree is evergreen—and long liv-ing—meaning he planned on staying there a long time.[19]

My uncle Robert, my mother's closest brother, lived over the hill and through the woods from us. He had a tiny two-bedroom house (where he raised his five kids!) and enough land around him for a huge, bountiful garden. A giant oak stood between the house and the garden. One of my most distinct memories is sitting on an old wooden picnic table under that tree one summer as four or five of my girl cousins sat with cubes of ice on their ears while chewing gum, their legs dangling—all lined up and waiting for their turn when they would place the gum behind their ears and Robert would carefully push a needle through so they would have pierced ears.

Later, when Robert had become the beloved community gardener with the best tomatoes in town, I learned by way of a full-page newspaper article that he had planted that oak tree when he'd built the house in hopes of hanging a swing from its limbs for his children to swing from. The picture in the article showed him sitting on a porch swing hung from a limb of the giant oak holding one of his many great-grandchildren. His roots ran deep. He had planted that tree with hopes of settling the land and raising his family there.

God blessed Abraham too. He provided safety spelled out in covenants and respectful relationships with the people living in the land. God provided land with flowing water from a well. God provided the promised son, Isaac, born of Sarah, his lawful wife. And God prepared a future for the outcast Hagar and her son Ishmael. Fear of God's amazing power and faithfulness is a good thing. Fear of anything else is useless.

Satan wants us to be fearful of everything. He loves to whisper in our ear that we should doubt God the Good Shepherd, that we should be afraid because we are not worthy of His love. Satan tells us that God does not see us or hear us and that He will not protect us or provide for us. But that, my friends, is a lie.

This is what we see in these small stories from long ago. Just as Abraham was promised a son, we eventually see the long-awaited birth of God's own Son, Jesus the Messiah, Lamb of God, who came to an undeserving world. Because of that, we have proof, like Hagar, that God hears our cries of distress and opens our eyes to see the Living Water so that we may have life. Like Abimelech, that ancient Gentile king of long ago, God speaks to us in warning, telling us we are as good as dead, and encourages us to make a treaty of peace with Him—a treaty that allows us to drink from the well and flourish under the branches of an evergreen tree.

Do you ever wonder how the story will end? Go ahead, turn to the very last chapter in the book—not this book of Genesis, but the book of Revelation. There you can read for yourself the story of the long-awaited Son, the promised land, the water, and the tree of life. Fear is banished and peace reigns.

> Then the angel showed me the river of the water of life, as clear as crystal, flowing from the throne of God and of the Lamb down the middle of the great street of the city. On each side of the river stood the tree of life, bearing twelve crops of fruit, yielding its fruit every month. And the leaves of the tree are for the healing of the nations. No longer will there be any curse. The throne of God and of the Lamb will be in the city, and his servants will serve him. They will see his face, and

his name will be on their foreheads. There will be no more night. They will not need the light of a lamp or the light of the sun, for the Lord God will give them light. And they will reign for ever and ever. (22:1–5)

God sees you. God hears you. God will protect you. God will provide for you. Do not fear.

16
FIVE CONVERSATIONS
Read Genesis 22

He couldn't have told her,
as he packed up and left that day,
of what he was going to do.
A donkey, two servants, and the long-awaited son,
going on a little trip;
chopping the wood he would need,
some rope, a knife, the fire.
How quiet he must have been
as the conversation replayed itself in his mind—
wanting to make sure he had heard correctly.
Perhaps silently arguing with God
that this didn't make any sense at all.
Perhaps doubting his own sanity.
Did the hours drag by?
Or spin by too quickly
on that three-day trip?
The telling of the tale
is completely void of emotion.

No screaming, no crying, no anger.
And the conversations are so very subtle,
you either gloss right over them
or silently moan with anguish.
Read them aloud, and you'll hear it,
the pain yet to come.

**The First Conversation
(Genesis 22:1–2, my paraphrase)**

"Abraham (I call you by name).
Take your son (that I gave you miraculously as a
    fulfilled promise).
Your only son (as if you have only one!).
Isaac (the name I gave him to remind you
    of laughter).
Whom you love (… and who carries the promise of
    all your hopes and dreams)."

So very carefully, God describes him:
"Your son. Your only son. Isaac.
    Whom you love."
Four ways to describe this precious
flesh-and-blood center of Abraham's life.
"And go …"
God had told Abraham to "go" before;
it was the beginning of this journey.[20]
Go away from the home he knew
and into a foreign land
where he would always be the stranger.

But that was the beginning:
what God was commanding now was the end.
"Sacrifice him (this beloved, long-awaited-for,
    miracle son)
as a burnt offering
on one of the mountains I will tell you about."

God knew what He was asking. He was telling Abraham to do the most horrible, unthinkable act that would destroy everything in his life. There would be no recovering from this loss. Can you imagine returning to Sarah, whose soul had ached for all those many years to hold a child of her own—and now her husband, whom she faithfully followed all over kingdom come, had decided one day, out of the blue, to murder him in some ritualistic, sadistic ceremony on a hill?

How do you think that would have gone over? How do you think that would have worked out? Would it have strengthened their marriage? Would it have deepened their trust in a sovereign (15:2), almighty (17:1), eternal (21:33), God Most High (14:22)?

What in the world was God thinking? What, indeed?

The Next Conversation
(22:5, my paraphrase)

"Stay here and wait with the donkey,"
    Abraham says to his servants,
"while the boy and I go over there.
We will worship and then we will come back
    to you."

This is where we find ourselves most of the time: waiting with the donkey—while God is working out the bigger issues with the Abrahams and the Isaacs of the world. We don't see the bigger struggles going on. We don't have to make the real commitment to die for our love of God or to sacrifice all we have. We simply have to wait.

But we are not waiting for nothing. We are waiting for them to come back.

That's the good part of God's stories to us—He always comes back.

Jesus came back to those waiting for Him in the Garden of Gethsemane as He prayed. He came back to those waiting at the tomb for Him. He came back to those waiting in the upper room at Pentecost. And He tells us He is coming back again with the blast of a trumpet.

"Stay here with the donkey, and we will come back to you."

And the Most Poignant Conversation of Them All (22:6–8, my paraphrase)

"Father?" Isaac asks.
"Yes, my son?"
"The fire and the wood are here,
but where is the lamb for the burnt offering?"
How do you answer that question?
The foundation of love is trust and protection—
how do you even think about destroying,
    letting go of,
the person that everything within you
    screams out to protect?

Somehow this journey that Abraham was on with God had prepared him, had given him something much bigger to trust than reality. He doesn't know the answer to Isaac's question—but this he does know: "God Himself will provide the lamb."

This story is one specific man's love and trust for his God—a God who asked one man to sacrifice all he had simply to test his faith. A God who had never asked for a human sacrifice before and never did again. It's just an interesting, wild story unless you see what it was preparing a whole nation of people to see and believe—another story to come, of a Father sacrificing His one and only Son whom He loved.

I think it goes like this:

"For God so loved the world that he gave his one and only Son, that whoever believes in him shall not perish but have eternal life" (John 3:16).

We forget that Jesus Himself spoke those words. Jesus came in the place of Isaac—from God's point of view. Jesus came as the ram caught in the thicket—from Abraham and Isaac's point of view. Jesus died so that we do not have to.

"God Himself will provide the lamb."

There was a struggle, I believe. There were tears and anguish as Isaac fought being bound and laid upon the altar, upon the wood. I don't think he lay down willingly or there would have been no need for the rope. We know Jesus Himself fought His Father's plan of His own sacrifice upon the wood of the cross. Anguished, His sweat fell like drops of blood to the ground as He pleaded for His Father to take the cup He was about to drink—that brutal sacrifice—away from Him.

I don't think father Abraham ever took his eyes off Isaac, his son whom he loved, as he reached out his hand and took the knife. Eyes locked, Abraham, looking deeply and lovingly into the eyes of Isaac—fear and love all tangled up together, knife raised ...

As the Voice Calls Out from Heaven Above (22:11–13, my paraphrase)

"Abraham! Abraham!"
"Here I am," he responds, eyes still on his son.
"Do not lay a hand on the boy—
I have provided the lamb."
And Abraham looks up—
breaking eye contact with his son,
to see the ram tangled in the thicket.
"God Himself will provide the lamb."
And He did.

But There Was One More Conversation (22:15–18, my paraphrase)

The angel of the Lord called from heaven above
a second time
and he made a promise—
a promise so big that it could only be sworn by the
    Lord Himself.
Because of this trusting,
no-holding-back relationship between
one man and one God,
all nations on earth would be blessed. All nations.
God would provide descendants,
"as numerous as the stars in the sky and

as numerous as the sand on the seashore—
descendants who will take possession
of the cities of their enemies
and through them,
these children of Isaac,
will come one Son,
who will bless all nations on earth."
For God so loved the world—
that He chose—at great cost—
to give, to provide, to sacrifice,
His own,
one and only,
beloved Son,
as the perfect Lamb
who could pay the price of the crime
for those condemned to die.
And instead of death, they would have
     everlasting life.
"God Himself will provide the lamb."
And He did.

This is such a familiar story, this small story of so long ago of Abraham and Isaac. Don't let the familiarity dull the horror. Don't think for one minute that Abraham had great faith and it made raising the knife above his own son easy. Do you trust God? Would you kill your own child to prove it? That would make you crazy, now, wouldn't it? It would be outrageous to think for even one minute that God would expect you to do such a thing ... yet it is exactly what we believe.

God gave His only Son. For us.

Let it sink in. It is unbelievable. It is crazy. It is outrageous. He gave us an unbelievable, crazy, outrageous story about a man willing to kill his beloved son—so that we would be prepared, we would be familiar with, we would have a chance of understanding this greatest story that will ever be told of a God who loved so much that He would sacrifice everything for a dying world. God Himself would provide the Lamb.

And He did.

17
SIGNING THE DEED
Read Genesis 23

I recently spent an enchanted weekend in the mountains of North Carolina. In one of the few box canyons in the eastern United States, the property was out of a storybook with lush forests, imposing rock cliffs, and meandering streams. In the middle of summer, it was twenty degrees cooler than the city temperatures I had left behind. We spent the mornings hiking the manicured paths through the woods, the afternoons swimming and canoeing in a crystal-clear lake, and the nights gazing at the stars.

I was there by invitation of one of the owners of this gated community, the brother of a friend of mine. We were also included at dinner at the "farmhouse" on Friday night where we mingled and dined with the other homeowners in this magical place. Each person there greeted us with warmth and hospitality as if we were old friends. It was almost easy to forget, for a little while, that there was one very large difference between us and them. They held a key that unlocked the door; we had a suitcase packed with a few days' clothing. That world belonged to the owners of the property. We were visitors in their land.

This, without us realizing it, was where Abraham had been all this time. He was a visitor in this promised land. He had pitched his tent there, grazed his flocks there, dug wells there. He birthed his sons there, formed alliances with his neighbors, fought their enemies, and built altars to his God there. But he had simply been a visitor—because he didn't own property there. After all these years, he was still an outsider in that world.

Then Sarah died. His wife who had followed him all over kingdom come, leaving everything she knew behind her. She had lied when he asked her to lie, pretending to be his sister to protect him from powerful kings in this strange land. She had offered her own handmaiden when she was unable to produce him an heir. She had borne the shame of being barren in a world that evaluated a woman's worth in the number of children she could produce. Then she had experienced the ridiculousness of giving birth in her old age. Ninety-plus years old and chasing a toddler around—can you imagine? Now she was gone—and there was no place to lay her body. Sarah, "royal princess," was a pauper without a grave.

Abraham was devastated. He mourned for her, laying his body beside hers one last time. Her eyes did not gaze back into his; her touch had gone cold. What could he do to honor this woman he loved? Where could he safely lay this flesh of his flesh and bones of his bones?

He went to the people of the land as an alien and stranger, asking to buy a piece of their land (Genesis 23:3–20). He needed land to bury his dead. "Oh, good gracious," they told him, "we will be more than happy to let you bury your wife here on our land." They all nodded their heads in agreement. Borrowed land, though, is a temporary thing. It is a suitcase, packed and waiting by the back door. Borrowed land allows no roots to grow. Borrowed land demands permission to enter and expectations to leave. Abraham had permanence and deep roots in mind. Abraham needed to hold the key in his hand.

He humbled himself before these Hittites. He bowed low, spoke respectfully, and refused their generosity. "I will pay the price," he insisted. "Whatever it is, I will pay the price."

Things of great value require a great price. Abraham was willing to pay a great price because he greatly valued this land where God had led him. This was the land he was to call home. This was the land of his future: Hebron, in the land of Canaan. He began his history with the land by placing the body of his wife within the cave at the end of the field in Machpelah near Mamre, Hebron. This was where Abraham would also be buried, as well as Isaac and Rebecca, and Jacob and Leah. It would become the family burial plot. When the Israelites returned here after captivity in Egypt, Caleb would call Hebron home. When David became king, he would rule for the first seven years from Hebron. Hebron, in the land of Canaan, would now be associated with the life of Abraham instead of Ephron the Hittite.

Interestingly the name Hebron is derived from the Hebrew word for "friend"—a description of Abraham, who was called the friend of God. The Arabic version of Hebron, *El-Khalil* (or *Al-Khalil*), also means "the friend." This is holy land for both Muslim and Jew.[21] It began with a promise from God and a grave for Sarah. Land signifying permanence, commitment, a future. Abraham purchased the key to the lock that opened the door.

Wars are fought for lesser things. But, indeed, wars are fought about exactly this: To whom does this land belong, this land with the bones of Sarah? It may surprise you to know that Hebron, only nineteen miles south of Jerusalem, is in the West Bank, under Palestinian jurisdiction. There is a Muslim mosque that surrounds this holy plot of land because the Muslims trace their connection to Father Abraham through Ishmael instead of Isaac.[22]

I am not sure how to take away a personal life application here. I don't know how this small story can make my life better or worse. Some things are told because they are history. It is interesting and perhaps noteworthy, though, that Abraham will not see the promises of God unfold. He will not see descendants that outnumber the stars in the sky. He will not possess the land as far as his eyes can see. But what he saw of this great God was enough. Enough to call a foreign land home. Enough to place his faith in God alone.

If we open the book of Hebrews, thousands of years forward in the New Testament, the writer there understood this story much better than I do. He wrote about the meaning of faith: "Faith shows the reality of what we hope for; it is the evidence of things we cannot see" (11:1 NLT).

He also wrote of Abraham's faith and Sarah's:

> Abraham was confidently looking forward to a city with eternal foundations, a city designed and built by God.
>
> It was by faith that even Sarah was able to have a child, though she was barren and was too old. She believed that God would keep his promise. And so

a whole nation came from this one man who was as
good as dead—a nation with so many people that,
like the stars in the sky and the sand on the seashore, there is no way to count them.

All these people died still believing what God
had promised them. They did not receive what
was promised, but they saw it all from a distance
and welcomed it. They agreed that they were
foreigners and nomads here on earth. Obviously,
people who say such things are looking forward
to a country they can call their own. If they had
longed for the country they came from, they could
have gone back. But they were looking for a better
place, a heavenly homeland. That is why God is not
ashamed to be called their God, for he has prepared
a city for them. (vv. 10–16 NLT)

Through the eyes of the faith of Abraham, we see God yet
more clearly. Abraham saw something so intimate in his relationship with God that he was known as the friend of God. He
saw something so trustworthy in God that he accepted a cave
and a field as the fulfillment of God's promise of land stretching
beyond where his eyes could see. He accepted the name Abraham, Father of a Nation, though only one son, Isaac, would be
called the son of promise. Isaac, miracle baby, would be the
only child from the union of Abraham and Sarah. Yet through
that line of Isaac, we trace forward to a nation and a Savior—a
Savior who will hold the keys to a heavenly home.

Oddly enough, that same Savior comforted His followers
before His death with these words:

"Do not let your hearts be troubled. Trust in God;
trust also in me. In my Father's house are many
rooms; if it were not so, I would have told you. I am
going there to prepare a place for you. And if I go
and prepare a place for you, I will come back and
take you to be with me that you also may be where
I am. You know the way to the place where I am
going." (John 14:1–4)

Do you struggle to have faith in God when promises seem to
be unanswered? Do you sometimes feel like a stranger in a foreign land? Or have you become a little too comfortable here?
Jesus promised to prepare a place for you. It is a home bought
at a great price.

Do you know the way there?

18
SERVANT
Read Genesis 24

Oh, to have the heart of a servant,
the thoughts of a servant,
the words of a servant,
the hands and feet of a servant.
Lord, teach me to be a servant.

Did you ever, for one minute, when you were little, dream of growing up to be a servant? I seriously doubt it. My dreams of what I would be when I grew up looked more like this: crown on my head. Yes, totally. I wanted to be a princess. I wanted to look like a princess, wear beautiful clothes like a princess, and to have everything I wanted, like a princess. I wanted to be married to a prince and live in a world that was pink and sparkly and fluffy like I imagined a princess would. Yes, totally a princess—that would be the life for me! A lot of grown women walk around believing they are princesses—and they are working hard to maintain the fantasy.

That is not the life God wants for us. Instead of a crown, a symbol of royalty, His desire is to give us a tray, the symbol of a servant. You will not find encouragement to take on the life of a servant anywhere in our culture. But God's Word, His book of truth, is filled with it from beginning to end, and this twenty-fourth chapter of Genesis is a beautiful picture of what a servant looks like.

Before we delve into this, I want to share with you an interesting parallel from this chapter for those of us who are Christians. There was the father: Abraham. Like God the Father, Abraham had the power and authority to send his chief servant out on a mission. There was the unnamed servant, who could be thought of as the Holy Spirit going out on behalf of the Father, searching and interceding on behalf of the Father. There was the son, Isaac, similar to Jesus, trusting the Father's plan for his life, receiving the wife chosen for him. Then there was the longed-for bride, Rebekah, symbolic of the Church—the body of believers willing to follow the Holy Spirit's call to meet her groom. Rebekah said, "Yes, I will go," and her life suddenly changed.

The Father, the Holy Spirit, the Son pursuing the Bride—isn't that lovely?

When I met Jeff and then started getting to know him, I knew something was different about him compared to any guy I had ever met before. There was something comfortable about him that I couldn't put my finger on until I met his family. His parents and my parents were almost the same age; both of us had been born when our parents were in their late thirties. I had older sisters that I had trailed along behind, learning about their music, their style of dress, their social behavior. Jeff had done the same with his brother, who was six years older.

The passion of Jeff's father was his cattle farm. My mother's father had been a dairy farmer, and my brother-in-law's hobby was his farm with his thirty head of cattle. When Jeff invited me to Thanksgiving dinner in small-town Alabama, I walked into the small shingle house overflowing with nine sets of aunts and uncles and a million cousins, with food lining the kitchen counters, and everyone embraced me and welcomed me. I could have just as easily been walking into my own mother's family gathering in Greenville, South Carolina.

When I found out Jeff had grown up in the same church denomination I had—with the same Sunday morning, Sunday night, and Wednesday evening services, and with both parents involved in serving in their church—I knew our lives had an odd parallel, a comfortable familiarity. Our families were coming from a similar place. Their priorities meshed perfectly. Deep down, our values were the same. It was a good match.

Abraham was looking for a good match for his son Isaac. A woman coming from a similar family with the same priorities, the same values, and the same God. He knew where she could be found. Just as importantly, he knew who he could trust to find her: his chief servant.

Listen to the command he gave this servant: "Put your hand under my thigh. I want you to swear by the LORD, the God of heaven and the God of earth, that you will not get a wife for my son from the daughters of the Canaanites, among whom I am living, but will go to my country and my own relatives and get a wife for my son Isaac" (Genesis 24:2–4).

This was serious. This was a huge responsibility. It was intimate and personal. "Put your hand under my thigh. Touch me. Feel the weight of my body. Be reminded of my bloodline continuing from generation to generation. Remember the sign of circumcision God has given us to connect us to Him forever. Put your hand under my thigh and swear by the Lord, God of heaven and earth, that you will do this."

How did the servant react? He clarified his mission by bringing up the worst-case scenario: "What if the woman is unwilling to come back with me?" (v. 5).

He was reassured: "God will send his angel before you so you can find this woman" (v. 7, my paraphrase). In other words, "You are not going alone—God is going before you."

Then Abraham acknowledged the possibility of failure: "If she will not return with you, you are released from your obligation to me" (v. 8, my paraphrase).

The servant had very clear direction in what he was doing including the repercussions of failure. He was reassured that their relationship did not hang in the balance of the success of the mission. Abraham trusted his servant, and his servant had security within that trust.

Next, the servant prepared for his mission. Becoming the hands and feet of Abraham, the unnamed servant took ten camels and all sorts of good provisions and gifts: gold and silver jewelry, clothing, costly presents for the family, as well as additional servants. These were possessions that would clearly show the wealth and prosperity of his master Abraham. The servant would arrive in a foreign land demonstrating the abundance and generosity of his master.

When strangers look at us, do they see the abundance and generosity of our Master? Do we present God, our Master, as the giver of all good things? Do they see the good gifts God gives—of love, patience, joy, peace, and kindness (Galatians 5:22–23)? Or do they see a stingy God who withholds good things from His children?

The servant also sought God's guidance—God's leading—before he opened his mouth on this mission (Genesis 24:12). "Show me," he prayed. "Show me clearly the wife for Abraham's son. Show kindness to my master Abraham." *Before* he had finished praying (love that!), God answered his prayer—and Rebekah appeared, with a water jar lifted high on her shoulder, ready to serve by drawing water for Abraham's chief servant as well as for his camels.

Now, this is interesting: the unnamed servant was looking for a woman with a servant's heart.

She was there, in the cool of the coming evening, to draw water from the well for her family and to carry it back to them. Think about how heavy water is—and then add the weight of a clay jar. And how much water can a camel drink? Aren't they the animals used specifically in the desert for long trips because of … what? Their ability to drink and hold a lot of water! I looked it up. A camel uses about five gallons of water a day and can lose up to twenty-five gallons of water from its body tissue without ill effects.[23] Five gallons of water weighs about forty-two pounds.[24] So let's say if Rebekah was drawing water from the well for ten camels, that could be *at least* fifty gallons of water! At least. If my math is right, in drawing water for all ten camels, she lifted at least a total of four hundred twenty pounds of water. Probably more.

This was no little offer: "I'll draw water for your camels too, *until they have finished drinking*" (v. 19, my emphasis).

The girl was strong. And willing. Look at her energy, her zeal. She *quickly* lowered the jar to give him a drink (v. 18). She *quickly* emptied her jar into the trough and *ran back* to the well to draw more water (v. 20). Then she *ran* and told her mother's household about these things (v. 28).

Do I serve like that? With that kind of willingness and enthusiasm? No. I admit that I don't. But after reading this, I want to! How exciting it is to say yes with enthusiasm!

This has made me realize I approach most jobs with a grumbling spirit: "I *have* to do this and I *have* to do that." I often approach my days dreading my responsibilities, procrastinating and putting them off. How different my life would be if I embraced my responsibilities and ran to them with a willing spirit instead of a grumbling heart.

Lord, give me a willing servant's heart.

Then we have the unnamed servant's telling of the tale. He told his story over and over again, and every word was a powerful affirmation of God's blessing and kindness, of his master's wealth and generosity. There was no guilt, no pressure, no obligation. "This is who my master is, this is what he offers, God has led us here to you. You are free to choose 'yes' or to choose 'no'" (vv. 34–49, my paraphrase).

Never think that the God who calls you to serve, to take on the role of servant, calls you to weakness or passivity. Though this unnamed servant was bound to do the bidding of his master, he had the power and authority and resources of Abraham. That is what God tells us about a life given to serve Him:

- "I can do all things through Him who gives me strength" (Philippians 4:13, my paraphrase).
- "Be strong and courageous. Do not be afraid or terrified because of them, for the LORD your God goes with you; he will never leave you nor forsake you" (Deuteronomy 31:6).
- "Do not worry about how you will defend yourselves or what you will say, for the Holy Spirit will teach you at that time what you should say" (Luke 12:11–12).
- "I pray that out of his glorious riches he may strengthen you with power through his Spirit in your inner being" (Ephesians 3:16).

Lord, give us the bold words of a servant! Lord, help us to be confident in how we represent our Master!

One night I watched a human-interest story on television of a young man and the love of his life. The program showed pictures of the man with his darling, vivacious girlfriend, who became his fiancée, and then the video of him proposing to her. They had committed to marry in two years, but the rest of the story was describing how two months before their wedding date, she was in a horrible car accident and suffered severe brain damage. It was heartbreaking. But I kept asking myself, *Two years? Two years? Why were they waiting two years? What was a higher priority than joining together in marriage?*

I don't know, but I am sure it had to do with something like finishing college or becoming more financially stable or making wedding preparations, or perhaps extended family goodbyes, as in Rebekah's case.

"Wait ... not yet," Rebekah's family pleaded. "Wait."

But Abraham's servant was clear of purpose, sure of his path, just as we should be:

> Give careful thought to the paths for your feet
> and be steadfast in all your ways.
> Do not turn to the right or the left;
> keep your foot from evil.
> (Proverbs 4:26–27 NIV 2011)

The unnamed servant knew his path. It was a path that led straight back to Isaac, who was waiting for his bride. And I love this next part (Genesis 24:57–58). In these ancient times— about which we often hear it was a man's world and women had no control—Rebekah's family said, "Let's ask the girl what she wants to do." True to her willing servant heart, she said, "Yes, I will go." So off she went, loaded with blessings, surrounded by her trusted maids, on a journey into the unknown, where she would see her husband-to-be waiting for her in the distance, watching for her arrival. He took her into the tent of his mother and loved her.

The stuff of fairy tales, isn't it? But it played out the opposite of anything you will hear of in our culture—because everyone played the role of a servant. Isaac had a servant's attitude: waiting and trusting his father Abraham to choose his bride. Rebekah had a servant's heart: she was willing to say yes: "Yes, I will draw water for a stranger's camels. Yes, I will go to this unknown life." The unnamed servant served well in word and deed, carefully and thoughtfully representing his master. And Abraham served God by trusting His character and depending on Him for provision in every aspect of his life. Abraham, Isaac, Rebekah, and the unnamed servant—they all served well. What a radical idea! It should stop us in our tracks and make us think: Can we live this kind of life, the life of a servant?

> Oh, to have the heart of a servant,
> the thoughts of a servant,
> the words of a servant,
> the hands and feet of a servant.
> Lord, teach me to be a servant.

19
THE STARS IN THE SKY HAVE NAMES
Read Genesis 25–26

This trail does not wind through our favorite stories. These are the chapters between our heart-stopping story of Abraham's obedience to sacrifice Isaac and the soon-to-be-told story of the less-favored son lying to his dying father while wearing a Halloween costume of sheepskin. These are the little-known stories of the ride along the way, so bear with us as we do a little housekeeping. We need to follow Abraham to the end of his path and catch up with Isaac and also meet the twins. In the meantime, it's like tidying up the kitchen: put the plates and teacups away, sort the silverware, and shut the drawer.

I have heard it said that men cannot live long without a wife, and here we see it in this ancient Scripture. Abraham, already an old man when Sarah died, took another wife, named Keturah. She didn't seem to have the prestige and position of his beloved Sarah—perhaps she was a servant in his household, but lo and behold she bore him more sons.

With barely a pause we hear that Abraham died at a good old age of 175 years. He had already sent his additional sons off

to a good boarding school back east, left all his earthly belong-
ings to his favored son Isaac, and Ishmael and Isaac were left
with the responsibility of burying Abraham in the cave with
Sarah in the land of Hebron. Good night, Abraham.

Meanwhile, Ishmael has had sons. Lots of them. Twelve in
fact. *Ah!* you may think. *This is along the lines of the twelve
tribes of Israel to come.* Interesting, huh? Ishmael's sons settled near Egypt and "lived in hostility toward all their brothers"
(Genesis 25:18). Doesn't sound good.

Then we peek into Isaac's life. Married to beautiful and
strong Rebekah, they had been together twenty years, but there
was no sign of children on the way. This was heartbreak. This
was great sorrow. Ishmael was reproducing up a storm, and
here we have Isaac and his beloved wife living in a home filled
with quiet. And Isaac prayed for his wife.

This is a powerful glimpse into their marriage: Isaac went
to God on behalf of his wife, Rebekah. This is kindness. This
is a hurting soul crying out for his wife. This is what marriage
is. Staying connected well into your marriage is a hard thing.
After the bliss of the wedding vows fades, the hard things of life
start to seep in. Finances are tight, in-laws cause turmoil, dis-
appointments stack up and tumble over. Harsh words accuse
and sadness wraps its coldness around you. The most important thing you can do as the rain falls is to pray. Pray for each
other. Pray with each other. It is hard to stay angry with the
person you are praying for. You aren't facing the pain alone if
your beloved is praying with you. So Isaac prayed, and oddly it
was enough. Rebekah soon had life in her womb.

Now it was her turn—she went to God. "What is going on
inside of me?" she asked. "The fighting within my womb is

crazy! It is as if this child will kick his way out of me. I see his footprint pressing against my skin."

"It is not one, but two," God told her. "Not just two sons—but two nations. One is stronger than the other, and the oldest will serve the youngest." Uh-oh, clouds were gathering on the horizon and the boys weren't even born yet.

Many parents-to-be, waiting for the birth of their child, will imagine the beauty of their coming daughter or son, and they will plan how carefully and thoughtfully they will raise this "blank slate" human. What they fail to understand is so very much of that child is already hard-wired in, and there will be absolutely nothing they can do to change those innate traits and personalities. It is as if by thought alone, they will be able to change their baby's blue eyes to gray. Or make a daughter destined to be five two grow to a model's height of five nine. Or make the quiet, introspective son be a lover of the limelight. God alone knows the way we have been knit together in our mother's womb.

Rebekah would bear twin boys. The firstborn was hairy and strong with a love for hunting and little care for anything else. The younger one would come out struggling to be first. Always strategizing, he would use any advantage to put himself on top. He would engage life to the fullest—wrestling against man and God. And after a late-night encounter with God, he would later be named Israel and become the father of twelve tribes. But we jump ahead of ourselves.

So they were born, these boys: Esau, the firstborn, Jacob close behind, holding tightly to Esau's heel. They were as different from each other as day is from night. Esau roved the forest with hunting on his mind. Younger brother Jacob was more reserved, staying close to home, training to be a culinary chef. We hear a disturbing fact of their family dynamics: Isaac loved Esau, but Rebekah loved Jacob. Oh no. This will not end well.

It is so endlessly interesting that God's Word is not whitewashed and cleaned up. We see the people of His stories exposed with their weaknesses sticking out. Favorites among parents! Everyone today knows we aren't supposed to have favorites between our children! But here it is—right up front.

Before we get too deep into their story, we see Esau's impatience and flair for the dramatic. He had been out hunting. Jacob had been home cooking. Esau burst through the door, ready to die because of hunger. "Famished, I am! Give me some of what you're cooking!"

Really? You are a grown man and you can't manage to feed yourself?

Jacob, with one sentence, revealed his nature and his heart's desire: "First sell me your birthright" (v. 31). The birthright of the firstborn was no little thing in those days. It gave the firstborn son the right to a double portion of the inheritance as well as the leadership role of the family.[25] Remember Isaac? He got it all while Ishmael got a shovel and the other boys were sent out of town. The firstborn was considered the one who would carry forward the family line, and along with it, all the family wealth and status. Jacob wanted what Esau had. Jacob wanted a future—he wanted the birthright of the firstborn. Esau wanted what he wanted now. Jacob was ruled by his head; Esau was ruled by his stomach. Esau sold his birthright for a bowl of tomato soup. He sold it cheap. He sold it quickly without too much thought. He left the room a poor man with a temporarily full belly.

A new chapter begins, and we jump back in time to see a bit of the man that Isaac, their father, has become. We are told there was a famine and Isaac thought about heading to Egypt, but God convinced him to stay put. God renewed His promise of land and relationship and descendants as numerous as the stars in the sky, as well as this continuing strange promise that through his offspring all nations on earth would be blessed.

Isaac stayed put, but like father, like son. We see Isaac lying to a king that his wife, Rebekah, was his sister. It was obviously dangerous to be a beautiful woman in that world. What is it about this scenario that bears repeating again? Sure enough, Abimelech, king of the Philistines, figured out that Rebekah was really Isaac's wife due to a little afternoon lovemaking. So the king placed a hedge of protection around Isaac, and by that time next year, Isaac reaped an abundance. Every year going forward, he became wealthier, crops producing wildly, flocks reproducing madly.

I can't figure out the takeaway here: Lie about your beautiful wife to protect yourself and God will bless you? That doesn't seem quite right, does it? Maybe it was the opposite: Isaac tried to protect himself by lying but was found out. He, by his own plans, *could not* call the shots. But once the truth of his lies was made known, God, in His blessings, could build Isaac into a powerhouse. The rains fell abundantly on his crops, and everything that he shepherded flourished.

It didn't take long, though, for human nature to rear its jealous head. There was the problem of wells again. Wells filled with freshwater were an asset. Every living thing needed water to survive. There was no turning on the faucet with cool water flowing out. There was no bottled water at the store. Life depended on finding enough water for each day. If you had a well, you had a pretty good guarantee of life. If the well was dry, you had to move on until you found more water. Abimelech's men and the local herdsmen in the area wanted Isaac and his entourage to move on out of their territory. Stopping up a well or refusing the use of it was a way to get them to pack up their bags and move out of town.

So they moved and dug. They moved and dug until freshwater flowed from Rehoboth to Beersheba and there was room to grow in an undisputed land. God came to Isaac again to promise His blessings. Isaac built an altar and worshiped and pitched his tent in peace. Finally, Isaac had found a place to hang his hat. Was everybody happy?

Oddly there came a knock at the door. Abimelech showed up to make peace because it had become apparent to him that Abraham's God was blessing Isaac. *If his God is blessing him,* he was thinking, *I don't want to offend him and bring harm down on myself. Let's make sure we are on good terms with each other and maybe a little of those blessings will fall my way.*

We do not live in a vacuum. We all live with neighbors. Others watch our lives and see how we react: how we react to fear, how we react to adversity, how we react to times of blessing and wealth. It is unusual and, dare I say, appealing to see someone who is at peace with life no matter what the circumstances.

Isaac was grounded in God and His provision for him. His peace was not dependent on the circumstance of clear water at the bottom of the well. His peace was in the giver of the water.

He could pack up and move on to a different and unknown land because God traveled with him. God was his provider. God was his peace.

One last little bit of setting up the turning point of the story to come: Do you remember back a few chapters when we heard Father Abraham's greatest desire for his son's future? "Do not marry the local girls." He knew the local girls, with their worship of pagan gods, could destroy his son's walk with the one true God. So he sent his servant back to the "old country" for a wife for Isaac. And here we see his grandson Esau marrying, not one, but two women—and both are Hittites. What's the assessment of those relationships? "They were a source of grief to Isaac and Rebekah" (26:35).

As a parent, I started praying for the wife-to-be for my son and the husband-to-be for my daughter when they were young. Marriage is not only between a man and a woman, but it becomes a joining of families, a splicing together of values. It greatly influences the children to come and is solid ground for the continuation of the family.

For a couple of years, our daughter dated a young man who didn't believe there was a God. She came to us one night after they had a deep discussion about their beliefs and reassured us they would never marry because she knew that was not the life she wanted for herself. Her belief in a loving God was the foundation of who she was. We were patient and loving to both her and the young man—and very relieved when they parted ways.

When she met another young man, who seemed to have so many positive traits that closely aligned with her own, we watched in amazement at his fascination with her faith. She turned down dates with him on Sunday nights because that was when she attended church, so he asked if he could go to church with her. He went to classes that introduced him to our church's basic beliefs and sought out a small group of men to join so he could learn more. He prayed with their leader to accept Christ as his Savior, chose to have an adult baptism, then married our daughter. Instead of being "a source of grief," he is a source of joy to my husband and me.

Family relationships. Some are lovely; some totter around on rocky ground. Do you ever feel like a family member or a neighbor is keeping you from having peace in your life? How often do you pray for them? How often do you pray for your spouse? How often do you pray *with* your spouse? Or for the future of your family? Do you trust God, but feel like He needs a little help making things happen? Can you trust God with your difficult relationships?

Families. God does not shy away from the messy relationships that take place within our families. And isn't it reassuring that some of His greatest leaders and walkers in this journey of faith struggled with damaged or broken family relationships? Problems of infertility, favored sons, sibling rivalry, trouble with the neighbors, and grievous daughters-in-law all seem to be old stories. In the middle of it all is God. Not surprised. Still leading. It will be interesting to see how this story will end.

20
BLESSINGS, BLESSINGS, BLESSINGS
Read Genesis 27–28

Sit with me as we listen in. We are hidden behind a curtain, hearing words not meant for us. Words spoken in private. Words of blessings and a future. Words of a destiny to unfold. More than a prayer, less than law-bound declaration, a blessing is personal, with hands holding head, heart opened wide, eyes seeing into heaven. This is who you are. This is the greatness that God has placed inside of you before you were born. This is where your feet will travel. These are the characteristics you have nourished and, because of that, how others will see you and receive you.

A blessing traveled, in this ancient Eastern culture, from father to son, in the voice of God. A father's blessing handed the future to the son. Or it predicted the dangerous path that lay ahead. These blessings we listen in on were given to Jacob under cover of deceit, and to Esau, in the throes of anguish. With a do-over Isaac would bless Jacob again, this time with honesty, as he sent him on his way, never to see him again. Under an open nighttime sky, with only stars as a witness, we will hear God's blessing on Jacob's head. It was this blessing that would ride through the centuries and land on his descendant Jesus, born on a starry night when angels would appear again, this time to announce His birth to shepherds in the fields keeping watch over sacrificial lambs. Blessings. Come and receive.

This family of Isaac and Rebekah makes us cringe a bit. "Really?" we want to ask God. "Couldn't you have painted a more loving family dynamic here?" Nobody comes out of this story looking too good. Isaac had his favorite son, so he called his eldest, Esau, to receive his blessing and excluded his younger son, Jacob. His instructions: "Go hunting for me, make my favorite dinner, and come to me so I may bless you" (Genesis 27:2–4, my paraphrase).

Rebekah listened in on this conversation not meant for her to hear, and so she called her favorite son, Jacob, in with a plan to lie and deceive her husband, the father of her twin sons. Oh, and they went to great lengths to deceive. Jacob killed two goats from the backyard pen; Rebekah got to cooking in the kitchen and added enough spice to make the goat meat taste like Isaac's favorite wild game. She pulled Esau's extra clothing out of his closet, and the next thing you know, they had carefully cut the hairy skin of the goats Jacob slaughtered to lay over his arms and neck. How did they attach it so it didn't fall off as Isaac caressed his son's arms and laid his hands on his neck for the blessing? I don't know, but they were up to no good, these two. And they were racing to beat the clock before Esau returned. I imagine Esau's bow had just found its mark. He knelt to place the still-warm carcass over his shoulders. Gathering his bow, he turned to head back home. At the same time, Jacob entered the tent of Isaac, tray in hand.

The conversation between Isaac and Jacob was riddled with mistrust (vv. 18–26, my paraphrase): "How did you return so soon? ... You claim to be Esau but your voice gives it away that you are Jacob. ... Are you really my son Esau?" Isaac asked point blank. "Come close so I can touch your skin. Come closer still and kiss me so I can smell your scent."

We know those we love by such intimate details: the sound of their voice, the touch of their skin, the scent that is their own personal perfume. Isaac was old and his eyes failed him, but he knew without a doubt the touch and smell of his favorite son.

When I read this passage, I don't believe it. I don't believe Isaac fell for the deception. It's my own interpretation, not based on scholarly knowledge. Maybe he wanted to believe it was indeed Esau, returned early from his hunt. Maybe he wanted to believe it was his oldest son and not a deception played out on him by his own wife and youngest son. Maybe he decided it was time to stop fighting the prophecy that Rebekah had shared with him before the twins were born—that the blessing of Abraham would fall on the youngest, not the oldest within her belly. That the older would serve the younger. So be it. It was time to place God's blessing on the head of this son. Whoever it might have been.

It was a blessing of abundance and power and protection from enemies, yet it was missing something somehow, but I can't quite put my finger on it. No sooner did Jacob, parading around in stolen robes and sheep's clothing, leave his father's chambers than Esau burst into the kitchen, pulling out pots and pans. We lean against the doorframe, sick to our stomach, watching as he worked, with him not knowing that what he labored for was already lost to him.

It is the part in the movie when we start to doubt our hero's ethics and begin to wonder if we should be cheering for the underdog instead. Jacob was a liar and a cheat, given unfair advantage by Rebekah, who loved Jacob more, while Isaac loved Esau more. Just rip this family apart at the seams. We hate this. We have seen those parents who dote on one child, while the other makes do on his own. We cry out, "This is not fair! This is wrong! This is hurtful! How can God let this happen? He needs to do something! He needs to make this right!"

We watch, helpless, as Esau went in to his father and all hope drained to the floor. Esau, though, was not the man we hoped for. We see, in his reaction, a man who blamed others for his losses, and we take a step back. No, this was not the man we want to follow into the future. This was a man who saw life through a narrow window of possibility and refused to take responsibility for his own actions. This was a man who played the victim card. Best to hang in there and see what God can do with the younger manipulative son, Jacob.

Esau's blessing was one of discord and a bowed knee in resentment—a heavy servitude of his own making. A life of excuses. It would take a long time before he could stand strong on his own because he allowed himself to be held down by grudges and plans for revenge.

Upon hearing of Esau's murderous threats, Jacob realized it was time to get the heck out of town. Rebekah, once again, had her own agenda, and so she went in to Isaac with a more appealing excuse for her son Jacob to buy a ticket on the fast train heading north back to her own hometown: "Ugh! I can't stand these Hittite women and their vulgar ways! (v. 46, my paraphrase). Now there was no arguing with this line of thinking. After all, Isaac's own father, Abraham, had sent to that same country of their forefathers to find a suitable wife for Isaac—the lovely Rebekah.

Jacob packed his bags and went to say goodbye to his father, and we finally hear the blessing we have been longing for (28:1–4). It is the blessing of Abraham. It is the blessing we have heard so many times before in this book of beginnings. It is the blessing of God Almighty. It is the blessing of descendants too numerous to count. It is possession of the land that God had promised for so long. With a kiss on the cheek, Jacob left and started his long journey to the land of his ancestors, Paddan Aram, in upper Mesopotamia.

It was a long journey, and it seemed that Jacob was traveling alone. One night he made camp after dark with a rock for his pillow, which sounds like a bad choice to me. In the middle of the night, he heard the most beautiful music, and then Led Zeppelin wandered over the hill, singing "Stairway to Heaven." Okay, that's not what happened. Actually, Jacob had an amazing dream. He saw a stairway, or a ladder, that rested on the earth and reached all the way up into heaven. Angels of God ascended and descended on the ladder, and there at the top was God. And God spoke to Jacob—with a blessing. Now, this was a familiar blessing; it was the blessing God had spoken repeatedly to Jacob's grandfather, Abraham:

"I will give you the land on which you are lying; it will be for you and your descendants. Your children and their children will become as numerous as the grains of sand. They will spread out to the west and the east, to the north and the south.

And something much more than that will happen: all peoples on the earth will be blessed because of you and your offspring" (vv. 13–14, my paraphrase).

Well, let's just stop right there. That is an enormous blessing. How can the lives of all peoples on earth be blessed by Jacob and his descendants? *All* peoples? This is not just, "You will be a good neighbor and people will be glad to have known you." This is not, "You will invent an amazing product, like the personal computer, and the world will never be the same." It is not, "You will discover the cure for cancer and millions of lives will be saved."

This is, "All peoples on earth will be blessed through you."

There were people groups on earth that Jacob had absolutely no idea existed. What about the Aborigines in Australia? What about the Eskimos in Alaska? The Mayans of Latin America? This is a crazy, outlandish blessing. All-encompassing. "*All peoples on earth* will be blessed through you." The blessed Jacob would be a blessing to others. How could this possibly be?

Jacob didn't know. But there was One who claimed to know the answer to this impossible blessing. His name was Jesus. He walked through those same wilderness lands that Jacob did. As a matter of fact, He was a descendant of Jacob. He seemed to know and understand things that others did not. He gathered an odd assortment of friends around Himself. Twelve of them, actually. When He was first meeting one of them, a young man named Nathanael—well, before He'd even met him—He told others about Nathanael's character: "Nathanael is a fine Israelite man who is a truth teller" (John 1:47, my paraphrase).

When Nathanael heard that Jesus had said this about him, he questioned Him (John 1:48–51 THE VOICE, italics included in actual translation):

Nathanael: How would You know this about me? *We have never met.*

Jesus: *I have been watching you* before Philip invited you here. *Earlier in the day,* you were enjoying *the shade and fruit* of the fig tree. I saw you then.

Nathanael: Teacher, You are the One—God's own Son and Israel's King.

Jesus: Nathanael, if all it takes for you to believe is My telling you I saw you under the fig tree, then what you will see later will astound you. I tell you the truth: *before our journey is complete*, you will see the heavens standing open while heavenly messengers ascend and descend, *swirling* around the Son of Man.

Jesus would declare that He was that ladder, that stairway, which opened the way to heaven, with God Himself watching from above, with His blessing. Angels had heralded His arrival on this earth, and angels would attend His departure back to heaven. As a descendant of Abraham and Jacob, Jesus would be the blessing to *all peoples on earth.* Jesus was that staircase to heaven that Jacob dreamed of so long ago. Jesus, the descendant of Jacob, was the blessing to all peoples on earth.

And then, so much smaller in scope comes the rest of the blessing. This is the blessing that Jacob would be able to see and touch because it would be so personal to him:

"I am with you. I will watch over you. I will be with you wherever you go. I will not leave you until I have done all these things that I have promised you" (Genesis 28:15, my paraphrase).

Now, that's a big blessing.

Jacob awoke from this night, knowing he was in the presence of God. A holy place. He would call it "Bethel," meaning "House of God." Jacob would return here again. It would become a place of renewal and worship for him: a place to remember the great blessings God had spoken to him.

Now if you have trouble believing the promises of God, you aren't alone. If you have trouble accepting that a God somewhere up there in heaven even notices you, much less has great plans to bless your life, don't worry about it too much. You aren't alone. Even with the heavens opening and the voice of God Himself making promise after promise to Jacob, look at his response: "If God will do A, B, and C ... *then* I will do X, Y, and Z" (vv. 20–22, my paraphrase). Something tells me Jacob wasn't quite trusting what God had to offer.

Jacob couldn't scare God away with his doubts. You won't either.

21
OUT OF THE FRYING PAN AND INTO THE FIRE
Read Genesis 29–30

We have met Jacob. The younger son who wanted more. The favorite son of his mother, Rebekah. The son who longed for more attention from his father. The young man who would bargain with a bowl of stew to take what his brother had. The young man who would lay goatskin upon his arms and neck to deceive his own father. The young man who had to flee his home so that his own twin brother did not kill him out of envy, jealousy, and rage.

Jacob, though, could not run away from his dysfunctional family—and instead, he ran straight into the arms of sibling rivalry—and an uncle, a male authority figure whom he had to honor and respect, who was even better at lying, manipulating, and deceiving than Jacob himself.

The hurt and the harm that humans can heap upon each other is laid out line by line. An enemy can hit you over the head. But a family member can slice you to the core. The closer someone stands to you, the deeper the knife can go.

This is the story of longing and hurt, lying and heartache—people so scarred by their own sin and the sin of others that it seemed nothing good could ever come from this mess. But that is the wonder of God—a God who continues to bless lives and directs paths to His glory.

We will listen to three different versions of the same story. The story slants and shifts its meaning depending on whose voice we hear. This is a story of love and jealousy. This is a story of greed and power. This is the story of two jealous sisters: Rachel and Leah. This is the story of their manipulative father, Laban. This is the story of Jacob, whom God placed between a rock and a hard place, to file off the rough edges and strengthen under pressure.

RACHEL'S STORY

My name is Rachel. I first saw Jacob at the well as I herded my father's sheep. Though I was young, my responsibility for the family was taking care of the herds.

In kindness, this stranger from a foreign land rolled away the heavy stone at the well. What strength! And he watered my sheep for me. Then, odder still, he embraced me, kissed me, and cried out, weeping, saying that he was my relative, that my father was his uncle. My life changed at that moment.

He came to live with my family and went to my father to ask for my hand in marriage—promising to care for me and love me. Since he had come to our family empty-handed, he negotiated to work for seven years for my father as payment of dowry. He loved me. I saw it in his eyes as he would pass by. I heard it in his voice as he talked with me.

I counted the days—one by one, year after year—until my wedding day and the week I would spend alone with him in our wedding tent. Preparations were made: wedding clothing sewn, special foods planned and prepared. Everything was ready; I could barely breathe with anticipation. As the sun set the night before my wedding day, my father came to me—and what he said turned my world upside down. It would not be me, but my older sister, Leah, who would become my beloved's bride!

My heart dropped, my blood rushed with anger, tears burned my eyes. *How can this be happening?* My heart ripped apart inside of me. My beautiful dress was now wrapped around Leah, the veils to obscure my beauty draped over her head. She was the one to touch Jacob's skin and receive his caresses.

I died inside that night.

LEAH'S STORY

My name is Leah. To be born with ugliness is a bitter thing. From birth, I have had an eye that wanders off into the wrong direction. Love songs are written about brown eyes and blue eyes—about how, gazing into their depths, a lover can get lost. No songs of love are written about eyes that cross or eyes that look off in opposite directions. I understood it from an early age: no one would ever love me for my beauty. I prayed and hoped for a gentle soul, a gentle man who would see what was inside.

My father loved me. But he was also a practical man who knew a good thing when he saw it. Jacob's love for Rachel was so overwhelming and strong—he would endure anything to be with her, even endure being with me. So that was my father's plan, a little game of substitution that basically killed two birds with one stone: both daughters married off to one good, hardworking husband. Problem solved.

I have to admit, I agreed to the plan. I secretly hoped against hope that a man with so much love in his heart for Rachel would have enough love left over to see the good, the worth, in me.

Our deceptive wedding night had its problems and close calls, but oh! What I did not expect was the tenderness of Jacob's touch and the power of his passion. Without intending to, I fell madly in love with Jacob that night—but not he with me. Love could not be easily substituted, and he still longed for Rachel in the morning light.

So has begun my life of loving but not being loved. I am duty and responsibility. My beautiful sister is passion, joy, and love. Jacob's face lights up when he sees her. He forgets to look my way.

I bear him beautiful sons, one after another. He loves the sons but not their mother. I give him my maidservant for his pleasure, and she bears yet more sons—but there seems to be no way to get into his heart or his head.

I love the man. I am obedient and longsuffering. I provide a welcoming home and raise his sons well. Yet I am an empty urn—unwanted, unneeded—and my sorrow aches within me.

LABAN'S STORY

I'm no dummy. I know a good thing when I see it. My sister Rebekah had left years before for a better life in the household of Abraham, as the wife of his son, Isaac. I'm telling you, she left in such a hurry that I hadn't had time to think it through. This time I wasn't going to let potential prosperity slip through my fingers so easily. I guess you know my name: Laban, grandson of Nahor. Everyone knows me around here. I've done well for myself: flocks of sheep and goats, sons and daughters. I've done whatever's necessary to provide for my family. I'm a good businessman, and I don't let nobody take advantage of me.

Sure was glad to see Rebekah's boy show up at my door. She'd spoiled him rotten. Thought he could get away with anything he wanted—and I figured it wouldn't hurt to teach him a thing or two. He was crazy about my girl Rachel. But I started thinking, *Well, if he wants Rachel so bad, it wouldn't hurt him none to take Leah too.* I figured he'd be good to her.

I tell you—that boy can work like the wind. He isn't afraid to give it his all when he wants something. Another thing: he has a knack of making things multiply and prosper. If you give the boy a dime, he'll turn it into a dollar. I like having him around. Makes my life a whole lot easier. I gotta admit, my estate has grown with him working in the fields.

Sure, I don't want to see him go. We're kinda birds of a feather, know what I mean? I know how to get what I want, no matter what it takes. Jacob is the same way—kinda like a son to me. I can't see him ever leavin'. No, I can't say I do.

It's completely crazy! How can God, who tells us He alone is Almighty God—and there is no other—possibly accomplish anything in this world with messed-up people like these?

Impossible situations.

Difficult, hurtful, self-centered people.

How hopeless is that?

God had chosen Jacob—strong-willed, manipulative, deceitful—and placed him under the authority of Laban, who was strong-willed, manipulative, and an even bigger master of deception, to teach Jacob who ultimately was in control of all things: God Himself.

God directed Jacob's path by leading him to exactly the right place. God alone was responsible for the birth of Jacob's sons—opening wombs that were barren and closing wombs that were fertile. God was the one who gave wealth—financial blessings of producing herds and even their colors, despite Laban's attempt to hide the speckled and streaked and Jacob's attempt to manipulate the speckling and streaking.

God was sovereign.

Not Laban, not Jacob.

Not Rachel, nor Leah.

Nor all their manipulations of their circumstances.

This is the perfect example of trying to herd cats. None of them were interested in cooperating, and each person was busy doing what profited them at the moment. Thank God that He is a master at cat herding! Ironically, God did something so amazing, and so below the surface at the time, that we don't even notice it amid the sisters vying for Jacob's attention.

Jacob had tricked his older brother into giving up his birth-right and had taken his older brother's blessing. But now he is tricked under the darkness of night into taking the older sister as his bride instead of the younger. And it is *this* messed-up story that becomes the story of the nation of Israel.

The nation of Israel would begin with one manipulative man: Jacob, whom God will later rename Israel. He would have twelve sons, born of four women—sisters and slaves— all of whom would form a strange family of favoritism and rivalry. These twelve sons would lead to the twelve tribes of Israel. It will be interesting to see from which of these twelve sons will come the line of a king named David and a Messiah named Jesus.

Jacob chose Rachel. Laban tricked him into marrying Leah. The sibling rivalry between Jacob and Esau was nothing compared to what Jacob walked into when he entered the wrong bridal chamber. I think there is a saying about hell and fury and a woman scorned ... and here they all are—just one big, happy family.

But God is sovereign. He can take the messiest, most impossible situation, and make something good and beautiful and pure out of it.

> He can take difficult, hard people—
> and in spite of hurt feelings and ugly actions—
> He can turn the world upside down for good.
> This is God.
> This is His wonder:
> all things,
> *all* things,
> will work together as He has planned.
> Nothing can tear Him down,
> nothing can pull Him apart,
> nothing can destroy what He intends.
> Out of the mess,
> will shine God's glory.
> Trust Him,
> and He will make all things good.

Can you relate to this story of Rachel and Leah? Have you ever been under the thumb of a man like Laban? Have you been betrayed by someone you trusted and felt like you could never get over it? How do you cope with unfair circumstances that you have no control over? Do you believe that God has the power to make all things right—that in His hands all things will work together for His glory for those who love Him?

God is no stranger to difficult family and unfair circumstances. Trust Him with your heart. He sees. He knows. He will make *all things* good.

22
BUILDING WALLS
Read Genesis 31

Something there is that doesn't love a wall ...
Before I built a wall I'd ask to know
What I was walling in or walling out

—"Mending Wall" by Robert Frost[26]

We are wall builders. We like barriers and boundaries. To keep ourselves safe, we build walls. To keep danger out, we build walls. To protect what is ours, we build walls. To keep others from taking advantage of us, we put up walls. We are wall builders, physically and relationally. "This is mine, that is yours. Let's put up a wall *here* so we can define our spaces." We like our walls.

Jacob and Laban were wall builders. Though they were living in the desert in tents with wandering flocks, they were both desperate to define their territory, their possessions, and their relationships. Who owned what? They had been hard at work for twenty years building walls with stones of anger and resentment and fear. It was an invisible wall but very powerful and strong: strong enough to wall themselves in and the other one out.

In this story of Jacob and Laban from Genesis 31, we see three forms of wall building. There was the wall of "running away" in the first twenty-one verses. Jacob built this wall with stones of fear. There was the wall of "hidden things" in verses 22–43. This wall was built with stones of secrets, deception, and unvoiced resentment. Then there was the symbolic wall made with an actual pile of rocks, which stood for a barrier of distrust and unresolved anger.

Things had gotten awkward for Jacob. It had never exactly been smooth sailing. Jacob had worked for seven years for the hand of Rachel, only to be tricked into marrying her sister Leah instead. His father-in-law, Laban, offered Rachel for an additional seven years of labor. Jacob found himself between a rock and a hard place married to sisters competing to be the most favored wife and the most prolific producer of baby boys. His father-in-law, who was also his employer, spent the following six years changing Jacob's wages based on the spotted or striped markings of the herds Jacob tended. Still, Jacob prospered. Laban didn't like it one little bit. Jacob's brothers-in-law were resentful of his success. Twenty years had come and gone and Jacob felt like an outsider in this foreign land. He longed for the home of his childhood.

God showed up. "It is time," He told Jacob. "Go back to your home. I will be with you." But fear entered in and Jacob took the coward's stance. Crouching low, he tried to become invisible by fleeing. He knew God was with him. He knew his success was so against the odds that it was God's hand that had multiplied his crops and given him possessions and family. Still, he was afraid.

God knows we struggle with fear. It is powerful and debilitating. It robs us of moving forward and moving outward. It robs us of success and relationships. It is not from God. It is a wall that closes us in and keeps us from walking with confidence in the paths God has planned for us.

If you crouch with fear and your trusted favorite defense is to run away, let's look at Psalm 91 together:

> Those who live in the shelter of the Most High
>   will find rest in the shadow of the Almighty.
> This I declare about the LORD:
> He alone is my refuge, my place of safety;
>   he is my God, and I trust him.
> For he will rescue you from every trap
>   and protect you from deadly disease.
> He will cover you with his feathers.
>   He will shelter you with his wings.
>   His faithful promises are your armor
>   and protection.
> Do not be afraid of the terrors of the night,
>   nor the arrow that flies in the day.
> Do not dread the disease that stalks in darkness,
>   nor the disaster that strikes at midday.
> Though a thousand fall at your side,
>   though ten thousand are dying around you,
>   these evils will not touch you.
> Just open your eyes,
>   and see how the wicked are punished.

If you make the LORD your refuge,
>   if you make the Most High your shelter,
no evil will conquer you;
>   no plague will come near your home.
For he will order his angels
>   to protect you wherever you go.
They will hold you up with their hands
>   so you won't even hurt your foot on a stone.
You will trample upon lions and cobras;
>   you will crush fierce lions and serpents under
>   your feet!

The LORD says, "I will rescue those who love me.
>   I will protect those who trust in my name.
When they call on me, I will answer;
>   I will be with them in trouble.
>   I will rescue and honor them.
I will reward them with a long life
>   and give them my salvation."
>   (Psalm 91:1–16 NLT)

When you read through that amazing psalm of protection, you see that when fear threatens to overtake you, God becomes your refuge and your fortress. He covers you with the protection of his feathers, as an eagle protects her eaglets. His angels guard you in all your ways. He loves you, rescues you, protects you, answers you, delivers you, honors you, and satisfies you. You are under the covenant of His salvation. Do you crouch low when you encounter life circumstances that loom large above you? Stand strong! Fear is no match for the strength of your God!

Then we encounter the wall built of secrets and deception. Before leaving, Rachel went into her father's tent and stole his gods: idols made of wood and stone. What a sad picture this is! And how symbolic! She hid them by *sitting on them*. I have to ask, how powerful is a God you can sit on? Then she looked into her father's eyes and lied to him about it.

How many times had she watched her father steal and deceive and then lie about it? And what did she see in her own husband? Was there deception there with the way Jacob had dealt with Laban? It seems like a lot of their business dealing was hidden from each other.

There certainly were a lot of hidden emotions—for many years—because they all came spewing out. Jacob was angry with Laban: "What is my crime? What is *my* sin that you have hunted me down like a criminal? Look at what I have done for you all these years! Look at how badly you treated me while calling me son. Look at how you are treating me now. I don't deserve this. I deserve much better!" (Genesis 31:36–42, my paraphrase).

Hidden anger or buried resentment doesn't go away. It grows. It festers. It builds into something much bigger.

And Laban's response? "*You* deserve? You deserve what? All of this is *mine*! Everything you see is mine. Mine, mine, mine!" (v. 43, my paraphrase).

Secrets. Years of secrets. Hidden truth, hidden feelings, and hidden expectations had done their damage. Jacob and Laban both had built a wall to hide behind.

What tears down these walls of mistrust and anger? There is a solution, written to people struggling to get along with each other. You hear it most often when two people are embarking on a relationship of love—but that was not the original intended audience. This solution was written by the apostle Paul to the church at Corinth because they tended to put themselves above the others around them.

If you are angry, hurt, or distrustful and it is getting in the way of a relationship, look at this passage with me:

> Love is patient, love is kind. It does not envy, it
> does not boast, it is not proud. It does not dishonor
> others, it is not self-seeking, it is not easily angered,
> it keeps no record of wrongs. Love does not delight
> in evil but rejoices with the truth. It always protects,
> always trusts, always hopes, always perseveres. Love
> never fails. (1 Corinthians 13:4–8 NIV 2011)

God showed me this passage a few years ago in a very few short minutes of time between two angry phone calls. At the time, I worked with two women who had a long work relationship that they'd mistakenly called "friendship." It was not. It was a relationship laced with jealousy and "You owe me" kind of thinking. And I was caught in the middle of it.

I hate confrontation of every kind, so my usual way to deal with it is to ignore it, hide from it, stuff it behind a wall out of sight. No, that is not a good idea. Because when you hide things, it forces you to lie.

So that afternoon I hung up the phone with one woman, shaking with dread because I knew the phone would soon ring with the other woman demanding, "What did she say? Who does she think she is? She has no right." Blah, blah, blah.

God called me to His Word, and this passage of love was where He took me. It hit my heart with power. Power strong enough to tear down the walls I was hiding behind, and it transformed my thinking. It calmed me. It filled me with enough love for these two bickering women that I realized *I was the problem*. I was making everything much worse by hiding behind a wall, trying to be invisible.

When the phone did ring, I was able to pick it up and lovingly speak the truth. I was able to say, "I apologize for any distrust I have caused, and for any part I have had in keeping things hidden. But if you have issues with her, you need to talk with her, and not me, because I love the two of you and I can't stand to see you angry with each other."

Do you know what? Everything I said was true. I could stand—exposed—without hiding behind the walls we were all busy building. It was so much better than hiding. That relationship between them eventually dissolved, but I was no longer in the middle, choosing one side of the wall or the other.

God tells us that everything hidden in darkness will be made known (see Luke 12:2; Matthew 10:26; Mark 4:22).

So finally, let's talk about piles of rocks.

Here's what is really sad about building walls: Laban spent so much time and energy looking for rocks to hit Jacob over the head with that he totally missed God speaking to him. He acknowledged this God who was so powerful and all-knowing that He could interrupt his sleep and speak personally to him in his dreams. He obviously feared the power of this God who could speak such a strong warning that Laban thought twice about how he would act around Jacob. But he missed the blessings of *knowing* such a God as this. He was more interested in missing idols that could be stolen, hidden, and sat upon. He cared about meaningless, powerless idols instead of a speaking, sleep-interrupting, powerful God.

What rocks are you carrying around that keep you from hearing God's voice?

Laban called on a heap of rocks to be his witness, missing out on connecting with the group of witnesses standing there around him: his family. He also missed out on connecting with the living God who spoke clearly to him in his own dream.

This is a cautionary tale. As we look at Jacob and Laban, we must ask ourselves: Are we running away from problematic relationships? Are we hiding our emotions and motives from those we are close to? Are we piling up rocks to keep others out? Are we building walls? Or are we tearing them down?

Ask God to tear down the walls that separate you from Him. Ask God to tear down the walls that separate you from those around you. God is in the perfect position to join together what has been torn apart. He can clear away the stones of fear, of secrets and deception, of distrust and anger. Throw down that stone clenched in your hand and allow God to open your heart.

23
STRUGGLING WITH GOD:
A MAKEOVER
Read Genesis 32–33

When I was a little girl, we always had fashion magazines in our house—magazines that belonged to my older sisters. I loved looking at those glossy photographs, and I read every word about the new favorite color of the year and how to go from daytime to nighttime makeup. I studied them cover to cover—they were my Bible. I especially loved the spreads that showed fashion makeovers; I loved comparing the photos of "before" and "after." I loved the way the experts could go in and change someone's hair, makeup, and clothes, and they would go from ordinary to—voilà!—spectacular.

As an adult, I still love the whole idea of "before and after" makeovers. For a while, I worked "staging" houses that needed to be sold. You take a normal home where people eat, sleep, and live, and do a makeover that will make potential buyers take one look and say, "Ohhh, I want to live here!" But the process of getting from "before" to "after" is usually a mess! Walls may get painted, furniture gets moved around, all the stuff gets pulled out and rearranged or packed away, and the house gets a deep cleaning all around. Things look chaotic and crazy when this is going on, but the mess must happen for transformation to take place. To go from ordinary to amazing, you have to go through the struggle to make hard decisions, pull out what is wrong, search for a better solution, and clean up the mess. It will be well worth it—in the end.

As we travel along with Jacob, we begin to see an amazing transformation: God started to do a great work in him. It was a holy, God-ordained makeover. Jacob had a strong personality, and you may not even like him very much. Let's list some of his disturbing personality traits: manipulative, self-centered, prideful, self-promoting, headstrong ... just to name a few! You may look at him and think, *Why in the world did God even put up with him? Why choose Jacob?* Well, God is in the makeover business. He alone could take those traits of Jacob's and transform him into something wonderful.

But remember what I said about transformation: it is messy—very, very messy. Especially when you have someone holding on for dear life to something they don't want to let go. And that thing they don't want to let go is usually control!

"I want to be in control of *this* because it means too much to me to trust someone else with it. I've always done it this way. I've always worn my hair like this. We've always used our dining room as an office. I've always had to make the decisions because my husband doesn't know what he is doing."

You get the idea. Transformation, going from before to after, involves struggle.

Jacob had been struggling from the womb. He came out grasping Esau's heel because he wanted to be first. Growing up, he wanted to be the favorite. He wanted to have the blessings and all the privileges of being first. He literally had to leave the country to keep from being killed by his own brother, and he ended up in another neck of the woods, with a different family, where he still couldn't help himself from fighting to have his way. He struggled with Laban because he wanted what he wanted *when* he wanted it and *how* he wanted it.

Laban, his uncle, had many of the same issues. So now we catch up with Jacob, as he went back to those problems he had left behind. It is interesting that he had to go back before he could move forward! He returned to his beginnings to face the consequences of his early struggles—and that consequence was the anger of his own brother, Esau.

The wonderful thing here is that God showed up, and that made all the difference. God had shown up before to Jacob. He had shown up with a vision of a ladder with angels ascending and descending from heaven to earth, and He had made a promise: "I will be with you." Over the years Jacob had seen that it was true; all his struggles to be in control were useless unless God was there.

He had left home as a young man, on the run and penniless, except for a stolen blessing and a birthright only worth the price of a bowl of soup. Here he was returning, preparing to cross the River Jabbok with livestock that numbered in the thousands, along with multiple wives, eleven sons, and a daughter in tow—and he was very aware that it was God who had caused this transformation.

Jacob sent word to his brother, Esau: "I am coming."

Esau sent word back. "I am coming too—with four hundred men alongside me."

Jacob was afraid. He had good reason to be. He deserved to be afraid. He had much to fear, for he had done much wrong.

Do you ever feel that way? Do you feel like your past could catch up with you and come crashing down and destroy the life you have been carefully assembling?

Well, Jacob did something powerful. And bold. And extraordinary. He prayed. And what a prayer! He knew who God was, and he knew God had a powerful history of being *with* people. He had seen it in the lives of Abraham and his father Isaac. He knew of God's faithfulness, and so he told Him that.

Jacob knew that he was small and powerless, especially in comparison to God's greatness and power. He knew where his success had come from: God. He knew he didn't deserve it. He knew God was worthy. He knew he was not.

He asked for God's mercy because he knew God was a merciful God. He asked for God's protection because he knew God had been protecting him all those years. Then he did something so bold—something that we forget to do: he reminded God of His own promises. "Remember, God—you said, 'I will surely make you prosper and will make your descendants like the sand of the sea, which cannot be counted.'"

Oh! Dare we expect God to keep His promises? Well, we should and we can! God does not lie. God does not change His mind. He is the same yesterday, today, and tomorrow, and His Word never fails (Hebrews 13:8; Luke 1:37). Isn't that what He says about Himself? Believe it. Pray His Word back to Him. It will bring about transformation—not of God, but of you!

We move forward with Jacob, and he went from praying this bold and outrageous prayer to sending gifts ahead for his brother. I see nothing wrong in this. He wasn't trying to trick his brother. He was trying to show him his heart: "I am not here to take from you as I did in the past. I am here to give to you, to humble myself before you. Here is evidence of my good intentions."

We are seeing a transformed heart. A heart that is willing to let go, to give, instead of a guarded heart that only takes. After seeing his wives safely across the river, he went back to be alone this final night before facing his brother. Interesting, isn't it?

But he was not alone at all. God showed up, and Jacob wrestled with Him all night—physical, arm-to-arm, leg-to-leg wrestling, muscles and tendons pushing and straining. It's enough to make you not believe the story—this ridiculous idea of wrestling man-to-man with God. Even if it was just an angel of God, I mean, really, have you ever?

Well, I know I have certainly struggled with God verbally, emotionally, mentally. But still ... If you have a hard time imagining the physical struggle, what's even crazier was the whole conversation between the two of them. Just listen:

"Let Me go, for it is daybreak." That was God speaking, as if a mortal man could hold Him back.

"I will not let You go unless You bless me," Jacob said. He realized he had hold of something much bigger than himself.

"What is your name?" God asked. Now I think He already knew the answer to this. Perhaps what He was really wanting to get at was the meaning of the name.

Jacob was was born holding onto his brother's heel. His name means "to follow" or "to be behind." It means "last of the lowest." It can denote the hooves of a horse, a man's buttocks, the rear of a troop, or the print of one's foot.[27] Not exactly an aspirational name!

"Jacob," he answered in reply to God's question.

"Your name will no longer be Jacob, but Israel, because you have struggled with God and with men and have overcome" (Genesis 32:27–28).

Since they were exchanging names here, Jacob politely asked, "Please, tell me your name."

I love the answer here. It gives you chills: "Why do you ask My name?" Because what was unspoken is: "Do you not know Me, Jacob? Do you not recognize Me, after all this time we have struggled together? Who could I possibly be, but your own God?"

When Jacob told the tale later, of the night that could have been his last, he would never forget seeing God face-to-face.

Why in the world did God spare him? And not only allow him to live another day but to walk forward with a new identity: "One who struggles with God and man, and *overcomes*." Now that is a God-sized makeover!

We have the same opportunity. We can take our messiness to God, and He will not turn away. He will push against our arrogance and our hard places. He will pull us out of our mire of fear and insecurity. He will not stop until the light comes into our lives. He will give us a new identity. We will be more aware of our weakness and walk with a limp. We will be more aware of His strength and refuse to let go.

We once had what a friend of mine referred to as a redneck dog. When we found her in the mountains, she seemed to be a mix of every scary dog I would never want to own. We would try to guess at her origins: maybe part Doberman, part

Rottweiler, throw in a little German Shepherd for good measure. We didn't know. She looked scary, but she was extremely sweet and intelligent. Our son named her Bisco.

My nephew also had a "found" dog, but she was a Shih Tzu. No explanation needed. They named her Lizzie and would bring her over to play with Bisco. It was fascinating to watch them play. You had this big black dog, strong and powerful, and this rather silly little pompous dog with pink bows in her hair who thought she was ferocious, with both rolling around on the ground together, growling and snapping at each other. Bisco would suddenly pause, her paw effortlessly holding Lizzie pinned to the ground, casually looking around as Lizzie continued to growl and kick her little paws as if she thought she was winning.

You see the same thing with momma dogs playing with their puppies, or momma cats training their kittens. There really is no contest of strength. The bigger, older one is teaching the younger: "This is how you fight, this is how you defend yourself, these are your strengths, these are your limits. You are the 'before,' I am the 'after.' I can take what you are and make it better."

God was teaching Jacob the same thing: "You struggle, but it makes you stronger. You can go up against the odds, and with Me beside you, you will overcome. I can turn your enemy back into your brother. I can make peace where there has been hatred. But I will do it in My power, not you in yours.

"I know you. I see you clearly. I know you have been Jacob, a deceiver, the last and the lowest, holding on to come from behind. But I also know who you will become: a man willing to struggle, unafraid to fight with man or God, a man who refuses to give up or to let go until you overcome."

Struggling with God will change you. It is messy. We usually fight back against God's changes, because we all like our old, comfortable ways. But God will not let us stand still before Him. He knows we must be changed into a new creation with a new name and a new awareness of who we are. It is the only way we can enter the Promised Land—the land where He is leading us.

Don't be afraid to struggle with God. It means He is in the process of changing you from ordinary to spectacular.

24
DIRTY HANDS
Read Genesis 34

One of the most amazing things I realized when I started reading the Bible for myself was that God clearly shows us the ugliness of life and especially the ugliness of His people. With skin-crawling truthfulness, flaws not hidden, the stories are told. Nothing is candy-coated. Nothing is swept under the rug. Everything is exposed.

We walk around in our world with dirty hands. Have you ever cleaned your oven? After Thanksgiving? We usually have a house full of people to feed, and on that day the oven stays on for hours. The turkey juices pop and sizzle and sometimes overflow as the heavy pan is pulled out. One year the grease caused the heating coil to catch on fire. The mess afterward was a mixture of black soot and hardened grease, and the oven cleaner I used to soften it just smeared everything around. I was up to my elbows in black gunk. Every cleaning cloth I used was so nasty that it had to be thrown away.

In God's world, you will find that He is not afraid of our black gunk, our dirty hands. When we are up to our elbows in the mess we have made, we expect Him to turn away from us, but He doesn't. He calls us to Himself so that He can wash us clean. When we have hurt ourselves, and others around us, He doesn't walk away. "He heals the brokenhearted and binds up their wounds" (Psalm 147:3).

We thought after Jacob had left his father-in-law's land, wrestled with God, received a new name, and made peace with his brother, that he would lead his family into a land flowing with milk and honey, and all would be right with the world. But that is not the way the story went.

Jacob told his brother he would meet him yet went off in a different direction. What is up with that? He pitched his tents within sight of the city of Shechem—which would soon not bode well for him or his family.

Now we have the dirty, heartbreaking story of Dinah's rape and of the slaughter of all the men of the nearby city. I think this is a complicated story, much like many stories we hear about in our world today. We have the facts, and we have specific conversations recorded for us. Emotions run high, and pride and honor get tangled up with protection and revenge as we try to read between the lines to figure out the truth of the matter. Let's dive into this heartbreaking mess.

First, let's say out loud that there is no question rape is wrong and causes great hurt and pain. No excuses there. Different words are used in different Bible translations—"violated," "defiled," "humiliated," "lay with her by force"—for Dinah being raped by a man named Shechem (Genesis 34:2), but the words and actions of Shechem don't seem to line up with what we expect of a rapist. I am confused.

We are told that Dinah, daughter of Leah and Jacob, had gone out to visit the women in the neighborhood, and it's clear that she was alone because of how Shechem took advantage of her. This "alone" part seems unusual to me—especially for that place and time. So I wonder, Was this a common thing for her to do? Had she been there before? Was she a frequent guest there in their homes, or was this the first time she had gone there?

In verse 2, we meet Shechem, the son of Hamor the Hittite who ruled this area of Canaan. Shechem saw Dinah, took her, and raped her. Then we overhear the most interesting conversations. Extreme conversations. It is immediately apparent this was not something done in darkness and hidden away. He did not kick her out of his bed and into the street. He doesn't come across to me as arrogant or demeaning. He comes across as a man in love. How much of the story are we missing? We never hear Dinah's voice, so we will never know.

But we hear something of Shechem: "His heart was drawn to Dinah ... and he loved the girl and spoke *tenderly* to her" (v. 3, my emphasis). Then he went to his father, the ruler of the land, and said, "I want this woman to be my wife. Will you go to her father to arrange it?" (v. 4, my paraphrase).

How would we know this part of the story unless it was part of Dinah's telling of it? Suddenly it starts sounding a bit more like Romeo and Juliet.

So Hamor the Hittite, father of Shechem, went to Jacob, father of Dinah, in the light of day and asked for her hand in marriage to his son: "He has his heart set on her. Please allow her to be his wife. Have your sons marry our daughters. Stay here in this land with us. Settle down here, work here, buy property, and build your life here" (vv. 8–10, my paraphrase).

Apparently, everyone around town knew what had happened between Shechem and Dinah. It was not a secret. It was not being hidden. They all acted and spoke as if nothing was terribly wrong. But not Dinah's brothers. They were shocked. Outraged. Furious.

So Shechem himself spoke humbly to them. He never sounded like a forceful rapist. He sounded like someone coming of his own free will to beg for her and to make things right with them: "Let me find favor in your eyes. You set the bride price— and set it high. I will give you whatever you ask—just name it. No price is too great to pay" (vv. 11–12, my paraphrase).

When her brothers told Shechem the price—which *was* too much to pay—he agreed to it, because he was so delighted with Dinah. Now is our time to cringe. We have to understand what he was agreeing to—circumcision. And not only for himself, but he had to convince every other man in town to do it also. Every man had to cut off—well, let's just say it—the foreskin of his own penis. Can you imagine? This was huge. And this was horrible.

Let's take a look at Dinah's brothers since they were supposed to be the good guys in the story. Remember, this is a story about God's chosen people, God's chosen family of Israel. When they heard what was going on at the outset as they returned from the fields, they felt great grief and fury (of course), but then they "replied deceitfully" to Shechem's proposal (v. 13). They took God's sacred sign of the covenant, the sign of a relationship with Almighty God, and they used it as a "business requirement." They bartered with it. They used it as a dare. They used it with the intent to inflict pain. Ultimately they used it to disable every single man in the city.

Once all the men in the city had undergone circumcision and were laid up in pain, Dinah's brothers Simeon and Levi attacked the city with swords and killed every single male, including Shechem and his father. They took Dinah out of Shechem's house. You wonder: Did she see the murders? Then, as if that wasn't enough, all her brothers entered the city and stole everything: the flocks and herds, everything in the houses, and the women and children.

And we are all thinking, *No! This cannot possibly be the way this story ends. This is horrible! Don't tell me that this is really part of God's story.*

It is not. But it is certainly part of this story—this very human, very horrific story. There is no happy ending. There is no moral of the story presented. There is nothing to make it better. There is no do-over.

I wouldn't have blamed God if He'd just walked away from them all, would you? "This doesn't seem to be working out too well, Israel. I think it is time for Me to distance Myself from you. Good luck. Out of here."

But for some reason, He didn't.

Instead, God showed up again, right there at the beginning of the next chapter: "Return to Bethel. Return to Me. Worship Me in a place where I first came to you and showed you who I was. I am with you and will watch over you, wherever you go" (35:1–3, my paraphrase).

We are still thinking, *But wait ... they all just walk away, with no repercussions of their horrific sins? What kind of God is this?*

This is a God who has a bigger story than what we can understand, and a bigger purpose will play out in the end. He did not abandon Israel because of his sons' evil actions. He instead called out to him: "Return to Me so that I can mend you and cleanse you. Come back to Bethel and worship Me there."

It would not be smooth going. Jacob would soon lose his beloved wife Rachel while she births his twelfth son, Benjamin. He would lose his father Isaac at the grand old age of 180 years, but Jacob would be there with brother Esau to care for Isaac in the end and see that he was properly buried. He would see his oldest son, Reuben, dishonor him by sleeping with his concubine Bilhah. All of this was nothing but heartbreaking— and disturbing. And we haven't even gotten to the story of his favorite son Joseph disappearing and being assumed dead. We haven't even gotten to that heartbreak—yet.

What will become of them all? To spoil the ending, I will give you this: Israel, as an old man, would lay his hands on each of his twelve sons in a foreign land, with twelve blessings. It would go something like this: One of his oldest sons will never excel in life due to dishonoring his father. Two of his sons will be scattered due to their actions of anger and vengeance against Shechem and all the other men of the city. Yet there will be one son of the twelve who will receive the blessing of the lion's cub and will hold the royal scepter and the ruler's staff. He will tether his donkey to a vine, his colt to the choicest branch; he will wash his robes in the blood of grapes. He will have a descendant who will be called King David—and a descendant who will be called Jesus.

How do you get to royalty and Savior from this mess of humankind? It is because God alone is our trusted Judge—God alone who knows the truth of the matter when our vision is too clouded to see. It is because God is a merciful healer who calls out, "Come to Me." He can heal what is broken. He can make right that which is beyond repair. He can remove the darkest gunk from our lives and wash us clean.

Can you trust Him when everything around you has turned into lies and deceit? Can you believe in His goodness when you are standing up to your ankles in blood and despair? Do you follow a God who can right the wrongs in your life? He doesn't cover up the ugliness of our sins. What is hidden comes into the light. Healing begins.

"Return to Me," He still calls. "Acknowledge your sins, and I will wash you clean."

25
TURNING POINT
Read Genesis 35–36

You may not have noticed, but there is no mention of God in the sad story of Dinah in chapter 34. But, as we already saw, God immediately shows up at the beginning of chapter 35, essentially giving Jacob one piece of advice: "Return to Me" (v. 1, my paraphrase).

Jacob had been on the run for a while from his brother, Esau, who was angry after Jacob had stolen his blessing. He ran to his mother's brother's land in Haran, where he met Rachel. His uncle Laban kept him running in circles between two sisters as wives, with infertility issues and shepherding flocks of striped and spotted goats to boot. Then he ran from Laban, straight back into the arms of his estranged brother, Esau— not knowing if Esau still burned with anger. In the meantime, Jacob spent a night wrestling with God and walked away with a permanent limp to show for it. Now his sons had left a river of blood in their wake.

When you look at Jacob's life, it would be hard to point at anything and say, "Yes, this guy certainly had it together and is worth emulating." He lied, he seemed to cheat or work things out only to his own advantage, and he ran away from the consequences of his actions. And look at his sons: they seemed to be following down the same ugly path—or worse! Are we sure God is with this man? Well no, we aren't, exactly.

God showed up again and said, "Return to Me—at Bethel." Bethel was the place where God showed Jacob a stairway to heaven, with angels ascending and descending. God spoke to him with authority and promises of a future: "I will give you *this* land. I will give you descendants as numerous as the dust of the earth. All people groups on earth will be blessed through you and your descendants. I am with you wherever you go. I will not leave you" (28:13–15, my paraphrase).

Bethel. It was the touchstone of God's promises. It was a tangible reminder that God was mighty and under every crazy circumstance had fulfilled all that He said He would. God was a promise keeper. Jacob now had a choice to make: keep running and resisting or return to the place of God.

Time to take a good look at yourself. Take stock of all the baggage you've been dragging around. And what do you know? There they are: those foreign little gods and symbols of fitting in with the common culture. For Jacob's wives and children, it was statues made of wood or metal or stone that they hoped would bring them good luck or special blessings. Even their jewelry identified with a culture that bowed down to little false gods.

It makes me wonder, What I have started holding on to that I think will make my life safer, easier. We all do it, don't we? I will put my trust in this wooden house, the status of this metal car, this glittering stone upon my finger, my gold in the bank.

What are the little gods that I feed in hopes that my future will be safe in their hands? What gives me that sense of security? In what do I trust?

Cleanse yourself! Get rid of your false hopes. Purify your motives, your thoughts, your heart. Strip off your dirty clothes. Pour yourself out; empty yourself before God and allow Him alone to fill you back up with His Spirit, His thoughts, His plans for your life. Jacob and his family buried all their fake little idols under an oak tree and then set out for Bethel to meet God there. Their enemies became terrified as they passed by— no one dared to pursue them. Instead of running away, Jacob turned to seek God.

Remember, back at Bethel, God had shown up with blessings. First on the agenda was a little name change. No longer would he be called Jacob, "one who struggles from behind," but now he would be known as Israel: "he struggles with God."

We ask ourselves, What? How is this better?"

We think to follow God that we must be compliant and easy—quick to say yes. We must be good little girls and boys who walk obediently in a straight line. But just maybe God doesn't mind the struggles we have with Him—as long as we are engaged.

We have watched Abraham laugh at God (remember him giggling, facedown in the dirt?)—and he was called "the friend of God." In the book of Exodus, we will see Moses push back and disagree with God when it comes to leading a group of stiff-necked people to the Promised Land. Here in Genesis we already have seen Jacob struggle with God—physically and mentally. And God didn't melt or sulk or fall apart or walk away.

God is big enough to handle our struggles with Him. He is big enough to face our disbelief and questions. There is a lot of freedom in that picture of God, isn't there?

So Jacob became "Israel." Now they left Bethel again, with Jacob a new man with a clean heart and open hands—not far from Bethlehem actually (ah, now that's a familiar-sounding town). Israel's twelfth son was soon to be born to his beloved wife Rachel. But a close walk with God Almighty does not guarantee a rose-strewn path, and sadly Rachel died in childbirth, but not before giving her son the name Ben-Oni, meaning "son of my trouble." Okay, we understand why she might do that in her death throes. But Israel understood the power in a name, so he gave the son a new destiny: "He shall be called Benjamin, son of my right hand" (35:18, my paraphrase). Israel would lavish all his affection on Benjamin and the other son of Rachel, Joseph.

With the passing of Rachel, we pause for a moment to see a list of Israel's twelve sons by their birth mothers. Twelve sons who would bring about the twelve tribes of Israel. We can't help but wonder: Which son among these four mothers will lead them into the future?

Leah's firstborn was Reuben. Remember, Leah was the cross-eyed older sister who showed up in the wedding gown of Rachel. Her son Reuben had potential. He would soon try to save his younger brother Joseph from death at the hands of their brothers by throwing him into an empty well instead. But Reuben would also make the really, really bad decision to allow lust to rule his life. He would sleep with Bilhah, Rachel's servant and his father Isaac's concubine, who was the mother of his youngest full brothers, Dan and Naphtali. Yuck. Basically, this was having sex with a stepmother. Not a good idea in any time or culture, so that sort of knocked Reuben out of the running for favored son in both Isaac's and God's eyes.

Okay, let's talk about the next son, Simeon, also born of Leah. Would he be the favored son we will follow into the future of God's blessings? Well, there was that horrible incident with Simeon and his younger brother Levi murdering their sister Dinah's husband and every living man in the city. These two brothers of violence would also be rejected as men worthy to carry the family blessing forward.

Moving on to number four son: Judah, also born of Leah. Judah would have—let's just say—an *interesting* history. It would be his big idea to talk his brothers out of killing their younger brother Joseph and instead sell him to the Ishmaelites as a slave, kicking off Joseph's journey to Egypt. Judah would have sons who weren't moral men—two of whom would marry a woman named Tamar. Then, through various twists and turns, Tamar would become pregnant by her own father-in-law, Judah. But we are getting ahead of ourselves. The good part about Judah comes later when he would step forward to offer his own life to save their youngest brother, Benjamin. And one day—far into the future—he would have a descendant who will give His own life for the protection and salvation of others. For now, though, we are still in the desert with Jacob, and it will be a long way to go before we cross that road with his descendants.

But be assured of this: These twelve sons born of four mothers to a father named Jacob will march forward in time and into our very world. They will go from twelve tribes to one nation. They will conquer and be conquered. They will carry the name "Israel" as a nation, the name that God gave their father, three thousand years forward into the future and into our modern world.

Jacob arrived home in Mamre, near Hebron, in time to hold Isaac's hand as he died. Isaac breathed his last breath at the ripe old age of 180 years. Hey! I thought he was on his deathbed years before when all this mess started between his twin sons Jacob and Esau—but apparently not. So here we are years and years later, and both sons were there to bury their father. Then we pause again to look at Esau.

I know this thirty-sixth chapter of Genesis looks like a boring list of names. Thank goodness for history scholars: hang with us a minute here while we find out what happens in the rest of the story of Isaac's son Esau. Technically firstborn and in line to receive the covenant blessing of God—though he was a twin sharing the womb of his mother with Jacob—Esau took several left turns along the way. His descendants would choose a very different future from that of their cousins.

As we've already seen, Esau married two Canaanite women who brought great sorrow to his parents. The next thing you know, he had married the daughter of Ishmael. We are not sure if this was any better, but at least this was a woman who had heard stories of rescue in the desert by Almighty God. But overall, Esau leaned into the influences of the Canaanite people and took up the sword against all those around him.

Esau also underwent a little name change, to "Edom," and moved into the mountains, where the rocky cliffs become a natural protection for his descendants' raiding expeditions. His tribe became known as the Edomites. The Edomites would show up again when Moses asked politely for passage through the edge of their territory on the way to the Promised Land. Even though Moses reminded the king of Edom of their kinship and promised not to touch their fields or wells, the children of Israel were turned away with threats by a large and powerful army. Not a very nice way to treat your cousins (see Numbers 20:14–21).

There is a teeny, tiny book of prophecy in the Bible named after the prophet Obadiah. By that time in history, the Edomites' reputation as mercenaries for hire was well established. They were there with the Babylonians when Jerusalem was burned to the ground in 586 BC. The prophet Obadiah delivered a message promising that the children of Jacob would be delivered to possess Mount Zion, but the children of Edom would be cut off forever:

> The LORD says to Edom,
>   "I will make you weak;
>   everyone will despise you.
> Your pride has deceived you.
> Your capital is a fortress of solid rock;
>   your home is high in the mountains,
> and so you say to yourself,
>   'Who can ever pull me down?'
> Even though you make your home
>   as high as an eagle's nest,
>   so that it seems to be among the stars,
> yet I will pull you down." (Obadiah 1:2–4 GNT)

Four years after they assisted in burning Jerusalem, the Edomites were overrun by these same Babylonians. The few who survived were gradually absorbed into the culture around them, and the Herods gained power when Rome conquered Judah in 63 BC.[28] A descendant of Edom named Herod would be around long enough to mock a descendant of Israel, dressing Him in a king's purple robe and entreating Him to perform some of His magic tricks.

Again, from Obadiah:

> "The day is near when I, the LORD,
>   will judge all nations.
> Edom, what you have done
>   will be done to you.
> You will get back what you have given." (v. 15 GNT)

When the Romans destroyed Jerusalem in 70 AD, the last of the Edomites disappeared from history.[29]

A little chilling, huh? Two brothers with two very different choices. We all make choices. Sometimes it seems like a small thing: "I am hungry now so I will sell my birthright for a bowl of stew." Sometimes our choices are so heartbreaking, it seems like no matter what we do, things can never be made right—and you are humbled to your knees: "I just watched my sons return with blood on their hands and plunder in their pockets—so I will wash myself clean and turn back to Bethel where God waits for me there."

Esau/Edom's descendants would fall far, far away from a forgiving God. They would eventually fall off the very edge of the history books. Jacob/Israel's descendants would fall down, yet they would get back up and return to the God who would be waiting for them: He alone could wash them clean.

Do you ever feel like the mess you have been making disqualifies you from calling on God? When you take a close look at yourself, do you find too much blood on your hands? Is it safer to assume that God would want nothing to do with you after the number of times you have run in the opposite direction? Somehow you are sure you can fix things up on your own. You can't. It's a sad Band-Aid simply covering a cut that will not heal. Turn to God. He is not afraid of the ugliness and the blood you have shed. He stands, mighty and strong, saying, "Return to Me."

26
DISAPPOINTING HEROES
Read Genesis 37–38

I have a friend who often seems to be going through a tough time. Her husband died from a devastating disease, she has an ongoing illness that leaves her exhausted, and her children are usually struggling with some difficulty. But the most difficult thing that has never changed over the years is that her family of birth stays angry with her, or each other. I have a hard time keeping up: if her sister is not speaking to her brother or if her mother is not speaking to her because of a perceived slight. My friend will often say: "I am just so disappointed that my family can treat me like this. I am just so disappointed." She is disappointed a lot. She really, really wants her family to act better than they do. But they don't. They seem to be unhappy people who filter everything around them by how it will affect them.

You may be feeling the same way about these "heroes of the faith" we have been reading about. "These are God's chosen people?" you may ask. "How disappointing!"

Why would God even want us to know all this dirt, all these sordid details? The good guys look more like the bad guys. This certainly is not a fairy tale—our heroes are too flawed. They make the worst possible decisions. They pervert and deceive. They intentionally hurt each other—especially their own family members! These chapters would be X-rated for violence, sexual content, and mature themes if they were scenes in a movie!

Are you disappointed in Jacob? Are you disappointed in Joseph? Are you disappointed in Judah? There is certainly nothing here to be proud about in the telling of this tale that plays out in these chapters.

None of this makes any sense unless you can see the end of the story. Luckily, we have this advantage. If we keep going to the end, we will see that these happenings were not hopeless or without redeeming value. Instead, they became building blocks of truth and peace and provision. Somehow, these tragedies, sifted through God's hand, would be transformed: "What you meant for evil, God has been able to turn around and make it good" (Genesis 50:20, my paraphrase).

We have three disappointing heroes here in Genesis 37–38, and they all begin with a *J*: Jacob, Joseph, and Judah. Genesis 37:2 states, "This is the account of Jacob." What follows is the account of his sons, and it is an incredibly ugly story. It is a heads-up for us as parents: our most long-lasting impact may ultimately not be what we do but what kind of parents we are. Scary thought, huh?

Jacob was a son in a family where the parents had favorites. His father, Isaac, thought the sun rose on his son Esau, while his mother Rebekah thought Jacob hung the stars in the sky. Their actions reflected that thinking. Jacob grew up and had a favorite wife, Rachel, and her son Joseph became his favorite. He made a special coat for his youngest son to reflect his son's special status, with absolutely no clue that his older sons didn't find Joseph so very special. Jacob had created a hothouse of jealousy and sibling rivalry, and every day it got hotter in there.

If you have brothers and sisters, you may have seen a bit of this ugly emotion in action. I am sure some of us could talk for hours about who was the favorite, who could get away with murder, who got the special attention, who Daddy liked best, etc. What incredibly damaged relationships result when we feel as if we are loved less than another!

Then there was the little issue of Jacob's name. Remember what it means? "He struggles" or "deceives." We saw that to indeed be his nature. He deceived his father Isaac to receive the blessing of the firstborn. His dealings with his father-in-law, Laban, were based on deceiving and being deceived; from the wrong wife to spotted or striped flocks. Now his own sons would deceive him by selling off their pain-in-the-neck little brother Joseph (instead of murdering him!). To make sure they properly deceived Jacob, they dipped Joseph's special coat in blood and hid their own actions. Ugh ... this story is so much worse than when you heard it in Sunday school.

But God changed Jacob's name to Israel. Instead of "one who deceives," he was now "one who struggles with God and with men and overcomes." We don't see that in him yet, though, do we? Right now we can only see one ugly decision made by angry, jealous brothers that would change the history of a nation. Are our decisions and actions in our little world that life changing? Are we that powerful? It is a scary thought, isn't it?

Then we meet Joseph. Most everyone has heard the story of Joseph. He is the exceptional young man who would save the entire nation of Egypt from the coming famine, and he got to have a moment of sweet revenge when his wicked brothers showed up in Egypt to beg for food. We get to watch them bow down to him, as he dreamed they would. Until we read the story for ourselves, we don't realize how the children's version of Joseph as a young man glosses right over his obnoxious personality.

Wait a minute! This is our beloved Joseph? He was a tattletale, quick to make his brothers look bad in the eyes of his father. He was arrogant and insensitive, completely unaware of how his words and attitude hurt others. He thought too highly of himself and too little of those around him, angering his own brothers to the point of bloodshed. But he was young, only seventeen, so God would have time to change all of that.

God began speaking to Joseph early in his young life through dreams. God gave him two dreams. Both were easily interpreted by his father and his brothers: Joseph was dreaming of his entire family bowing down to him. This was an ugly thing for them to hear—especially in that culture and in this already jealous family dynamic. I have a feeling that young and naïve Joseph didn't realize the hornet's nest he was stirring up. So off he went, whistling a happy tune, later traveling across hill and dale to check up on his older brothers' well-being at his father's request. The details were specific and something only Joseph would know: the brothers had moved on from near Shechem to Dothan, a passerby explained—and you have to wonder what was significant about these details.

I love it when God includes these little facts within these stories—establishes them in place and time and gives them history and meaning. Although the brothers had moved on beyond the tragic story of Dinah and the slaughter of the men of Shechem, they hadn't put enough distance between them and the horror of their actions. Did their physical closeness to Shechem reflect a lingering stain from the innocent blood they'd so callously shed?

We also have the brothers' conversation recorded, as they saw Joseph approaching from a long way off. Their hatred burned at the sight of him, so small in the distance. Older brother Reuben talked them out of killing him, Judah convinced them to sell him instead, and the best defense they could muster for this tattletale arrogant favorite son was: "After all, he is our *brother*, our own flesh and blood" (37:27, my emphasis). Family!

Do you have family that you would contemplate selling off to traveling merchants? Family that you wouldn't mind too much if they found themselves far, far away in a foreign land with little chance of ever showing up again at Thanksgiving dinner? By the time these older brothers sold Joseph off for twenty shekels of silver to their distant cousins, the Ishmaelites, and then dipped his beautiful coat in blood, Joseph had been reduced from "our brother" to "Jacob's own son." They put a little more distance emotionally between themselves and Joseph. It was as if they had already killed their relationship of brotherhood, and he was simply "Jacob's son."

There is an interesting parallel here: Joseph was betrayed for silver by a brother, an innocent animal was slaughtered, and his kingly robe—symbolizing a favored son—was dipped in its blood. He was mourned by his father and his brothers as dead. I can't help but think of Jesus: betrayed by someone close to Him—so close that He could kiss Judas goodbye on the cheek as he clutched silver shekels in his hand. Jesus's robe was removed as He was slaughtered, then He went down into the grave and was mourned as dead. "For God so loved the world that He gave His Son, His only Son" (John 3:16, my paraphrase).

For both Joseph and Jesus, this should have been the end of the story. But it was not. The story wasn't finished yet. Joseph would be seen again, this time in royal robes and standing in authority with the ability to decide life or death for those kneeling before him. We have it on good authority that Jesus will do the same.

Since we have this amazing story of Joseph and his coat of many colors and his trip to Egypt, I always thought he was an ancestor of Jesus. But he was not. Instead, he was the means God used to take His chosen people out of the Promised Land and into a land of captivity—for their own protection. They had already started intermarrying with the Canaanites, so staying where they had been would have led to these chosen people becoming indistinguishable from everyone else around them. In a land as foreign as Egypt, especially as slaves, they would be unified as a distinct group of people.

Through the brothers' horribly selfish act of selling Joseph into slavery, God prepared Joseph to selflessly provide for the nation of Egypt, as well as anyone who came there looking for provision. The "anyone" who came there would be Joseph's entire family: his father Jacob, his brothers, and all their future descendants. The twelve tribes of Jacob, those descendants of Abraham, would end up in this land of captivity for four hundred years, just as God prophesied at the beginning of this adventure.

God's protection of Joseph was God's protection of the future descendants of Israel. They were sold into slavery so that God could work out their salvation. Here—in the middle of the telling of Joseph's tale—we meet the brother Judah, who suggested they sell Joseph instead of murdering him. We pause to hear more about the sordid tale of Judah and his sons and their relationship with a woman named Tamar.

Judah married a Canaanite woman, and they had three sons. He found a wife named Tamar for his firstborn son, Er. But Er was wicked in God's sight, and the Lord put him to death. As was the custom of the time, the second son, Onan, took Tamar as his wife, and we find a fascinating description of his version of wickedness. It was ancient birth control. You see, he didn't want his wife to conceive a child by him because his son would be considered his dead older brother's son. So here it is, written in ink in the Holy Scriptures for all to see: Whenever he lay with Tamar, his brother's wife (who was now his wife), Onan spilled his semen on the ground (Genesis 38:9). This put a whole new spin on "what is done in secret will be brought into the light of day" (Luke 8:17, my paraphrase).

How would you like it if such little details about your life were broadcast for all to know? It makes us cringe a bit, doesn't it?

Apparently, God didn't like Onan's actions one bit and, judging this second son of Judah to be wicked in His sight, put him to death. By this time Judah was getting nervous about the situation and told Tamar, "Go on home—I'll call you later when my youngest son is old enough to marry" (Genesis 38:11, my paraphrase).

This all sounds so creepy and weird to us, but it was the tradition of the culture. You see, it was the responsibility of the men to make sure that the women they took in as their wives continued the family line by bearing children. It was protection and provision for women as honorable wives. It was a promise made by the husband to the wife. If the husband could not keep his promise, his family stepped in to keep it for him. Judah's family, therefore, had a responsibility to Tamar, but Judah had just lost two sons and he was becoming superstitious that *she* was the problem. He didn't want to lose his third son. He had no plans of calling her back. She was thus powerless in this situation, in that culture. She was destined to wear widow's clothing until she was taken in as the wife of the third son.

The years passed. Tamar was not getting any younger, and there she was, still living in her father's house, wearing black—not as a fashion statement but as an aging widow with no hope in sight of marriage and children. Judah's wife died, and it was a small town where news traveled fast. Rumor had it that Judah was going to take a trip to have his sheep sheared and that he'd be passing nearby where Tamar lived. So Tamar planned to have a "conversation" with him.

The creep factor just intensifies right off the charts. We have to ask ourselves how desperate she must have been to make this decision. How little hope was she embracing in her lonely arms to reach out for this distant possibility? What was she thinking? Maybe something like this:

I will take off my widow's clothing of black and dress as a prostitute instead. I will play the seductress to have sex with an old man, my own father-in-law, in hope of the remote possibility that I will conceive his child. When it is discovered I am pregnant, I will be accused of adultery and be condemned to death ... unless I can prove he's the father of my child.

This was complete and utter desperation. She put on the veil.

Along came Judah.

We look at him and think, *Whoa, Judah! Do you really not notice this red flag of danger flying over your head? What in the world are you doing? Aren't you of the family of Jacob, worshiper of the one true God? What in the world are you doing talking to a temple prostitute in the first place? What kind of life are you living?* Like son, like father, and we can quote that same truth of what is done in darkness will be brought out into the light of day for all to see ... but it is already too late.

Because Tamar had a plan. She wouldn't take credit cards from Judah, but she would take his promise of payment. So she negotiated with him to hand over his seal and its cord and his staff: Personal possessions he needed to do business. Personal possessions that identified him. There was no way she would have possessed them unless he had given them to her. Thus they were proof of an intimate, consensual relationship.

Judah had sex with her. Unbelievably she became pregnant. He went on his way, never realizing she was his own daughter-in-law. Three months later, when it became known that Tamar had become pregnant, Judah pronounced judgment on her for living an immoral life—an adulterous life.

"Burn her!" Judah cried, outraged.

In response to hearing Judah's pronouncement, Tamar sent a message back to him, along with the items he'd given to her: "The father of my unborn child is the man whom these things belong to. See if you recognize them."

Can you imagine? Desperation so deep that Tamar—the Canaanite woman, married and widowed two times—would disguise herself to sleep with her own father-in-law to carry on her husband's family line? The line of Jacob. Through the line of Judah. And she would make sure she had proof of the lineage of the child she carried. What a mess of family relationships. But the story doesn't end there.

If you flip forward roughly fifteen hundred years to the story told in Matthew 1, you read: "A record of the genealogy of Jesus Christ the son of David, the son of Abraham," and then it comes: "Jacob the father of Judah and his brothers, Judah the father of Perez and Zerah, *whose mother was Tamar*, Perez the father of Hezron" (vv. 1–3, my emphasis). Perez was one of the twins conceived by Tamar when she was disguised behind the veil of a temple prostitute. Unbelievably it would be Tamar the jilted widow and Judah her father-in-law who would together become ancestors of Jesus.

Just pause a moment and let that sink in.

Are you disappointed? Do you wish God's heroes were a little "better" than these deceitful, conniving people we keep reading about? It's a motley crew: Struggling Jacob and his murderous, thieving sons. Arrogant, self-centered Joseph. And Judah.

Judah: who had the bright idea to sell his own brother. Judah: who married a Canaanite woman and found more of the same for his sons. Judah: who had sex with a supposed temple prostitute who turned out to be his own daughter-in-law.

This, my dear friends, is the family of Jesus. This is the family God chose to entrust His Son to—His one and only Son.

I ask again: Are you disappointed? Do you think God is afraid of our messy, disappointing lives? He can take our struggles. He can take our deceit and turn it upside down and inside out. We will struggle with God; we will struggle with our fellow man. We cannot overcome this world. But there is One who could—and did. He was the descendant of Jacob and Judah and an outsider named Tamar.

Tamar's descendant Jesus would come into this world in His own messy way. There would be whispers in town of His mother Mary becoming pregnant long before her wedding day. She should have been stoned or shunned by that carpenter Joseph, but for some reason, he married her instead.

This Jesus would grow up to push against the teachings of the local rabbis and would rather hang out with sinners and tax collectors and prostitutes—and all the while keep the status quo on edge. He wouldn't listen to the wisdom of His mother and His brothers but would keep the crowds stirred up with outrageous claims like, "I did not come to bring peace, but a sword" (Matthew 10:34). Though He was the hope of the people for a few short minutes, He would die in shame at an early age on a Roman cross. Those who stuck around long enough to watch would look on in shock, disappointed to the core.

His best friends would remember the night before He died as the lamplight flickered against the walls and they shared a Passover dinner with Him—and especially His unusual words: "I have told you these things, so that *in me* you may have peace. In this world you will have trouble. But take heart! I have overcome the world" (John 16:33). Peace—or a sword? How could this story ever end well with this pierced descendant of Jacob and Judah hanging dead on a cross?

That part of Jesus's story would have been disappointing to His friends and followers. Unless, of course, you had time to wait around for a few days to see what would happen next.

27
JOSEPH AND A NEW ATTITUDE
Read Genesis 39–40

When I first read over these two chapters, I had just one question: *What happened to Joseph's pride?* Last time we saw him, he was an arrogant young man parading around in his coat of many colors and tattling on his brothers and sharing dreams that had his whole family bowing down to him. What happened to his pride? It was the main problem that led to being sold into slavery in the first place—which was actually an improvement on his brothers' original intentions to kill him!

Pride was suddenly gone. Gone. I think sometimes God places us in situations—surrounds us with circumstances—to transform us and to change us into who He wants us to be. For Joseph, his pride was a problem, so God allowed him to be stripped down. He was stripped down physically from the special robe of a favored son to the nakedness of a slave. He was stripped of his freedom to roam the countryside and instead led away as a slave, shackled in chains. He was stripped of a large extended family and became a stranger in a strange land.

His world turned upside down one dusty afternoon. There was nothing written about his journey from his homeland to Egypt, but something huge happened along the way: His pride was stripped away. He let it go.

I have heard that "everything changes all the time"—which is sort of a good thing. If you don't like where you are, don't worry—it will change. And if you like where you are, don't be surprised—because it will change.

Joseph's life changed in extreme ways. Extreme.

But his reaction became the same: *God is with me, so I am going to be the very best I can be no matter what the situation.*

This attitude was huge!

Think of the worst-case scenario of any situation you could be in—or you are in—a hopeless situation. Complete despair. There is no way you can affect or overturn the situation or its outcome. You are powerless. Well, that's where Joseph was. He was in a hopeless situation, and he was powerless—but God was not.

Somewhere along the way, Joseph became God centered instead of self-centered, and it became the most pivotal event in his life, with his new attitude becoming a blessing that spilled over into the lives around him. It was certainly evident in Potiphar's household. It was evident in the Egyptian prison. It was evident in Joseph's kindness to the cupbearer and the baker.

Joseph's life was centered on the Lord, so nothing could throw him off balance: not sexually compromising circumstances, not being wrongfully accused, not injustice, not imprisonment, and not broken promises. Many years later David would write, "I keep my eyes always on the LORD. With him at my right hand, I will not be shaken" (Psalm 16:8 NIV

2011). In the same way, God was with Joseph and Joseph was with God.

After Joseph's own brothers had sold him into slavery, he soon found himself in Potiphar's household. Now Potiphar was one of Pharaoh's officials: the captain of the palace guard. Think of him as the chief of security for the president. We read, "The LORD was with Joseph so that he prospered. When his master saw that the LORD was with him and that the LORD gave him success in everything he did, [*then*] Joseph found favor," and Potiphar "entrusted to his care *everything he owned*" (Genesis 39:2–6, my emphasis). The house. The fields. The finances. That is a lot of responsibility. Notice the sequence of events. I added the word "then" so that we realize that Joseph's relationship with God came first.

The Lord was with Joseph and he prospered. He was one of many servants, I am sure, but he stood out because of what the Lord was doing in his life. Joseph was serving others. He was a slave. Yet it was so obvious that he was trustworthy—and he was soon entrusted with everything in his immediate world. His master Potiphar gave a slave the keys to his home: "I trust you. I entrust everything I have to your care." Wow.

Interestingly, Joseph's commitment was not to Potiphar as much as it was to God. That is important. Isn't that what should happen with us? Shouldn't it be obvious to those around us that He's with us, blessing us in all we do—even if it is mopping the floors or letting someone else go first in line? God calls us to serve loyally, whether our masters are kind and just or harsh and unjust. "Submit to your masters with all respect" (1 Peter 2:18, my paraphrase). *Thank goodness I don't have a master*, you may be thinking about now. Well, almost all of us report to someone at work. So you aren't off the hook yet. It is so easy to justify our bad actions because of another person's actions. But that is not what God has in mind for us.

Joseph, minding his own business, found himself in a situation where another person's bad actions could have easily seduced him into taking his eyes off God. The house was quiet that afternoon. Potiphar's wife was beautiful and seductive as she chatted with Joseph, and her laughter filled the air. She stood too close, her hand rested on his arm. He could feel her soft breath on his skin. No one was around. No one would know.

Joseph could easily have justified reaching out to take her in his arms. Did his mind race through all the excuses he could give?

"I slept with your wife:
... because *she* seduced me.
... because I could gain more privileges with her favor.
... because I didn't want to make her mad and suffer under her anger.
... because no one was there and I didn't think I would get caught.
... because she obviously needs more attention and you aren't giving it to her."

Excuses. Self-justification. That is our easy way out.

Instead, Joseph called it what it would have been: sin against God. Remember, Joseph's loyalty was to God first. Giving in to Potiphar's wife would have been saying, "God, You haven't given me enough, so I'm going to take this for myself."

But Joseph's concerns were no longer focused on himself—his concern was only to please God.

Pastor Rick Warren wrote, "God's ultimate goal for your life on earth is not comfort, but character development."[30] God was certainly developing Joseph's character!

I love the way Paul said it in his letter to the Romans:

> Don't become so well adjusted to your culture that you fit into it without even thinking. Instead, fix your attention on God. You'll be changed from the inside out. ... Unlike the culture around you, always dragging you down to its level of immaturity, God brings the best out of you, develops well-formed maturity in you. (12:2 MSG)

Joseph was loyal to God. And loyal to Potiphar. And he ended up in prison for it anyway, thanks to the false testimony of Potiphar's wife! Well, that certainly didn't seem to end well, did it? Actually, Joseph should have lost his life immediately for such a transgression. Either Potiphar knew his wife well, or he knew Joseph well—maybe a little of both. So once again, instead of a death sentence, Joseph was taken away in chains. This was starting to be a familiar situation for our young Joseph!

The Lord and Joseph go off to prison together. Joseph was not alone; the Lord was with him. In the darkness Joseph became light. Even behind locked doors Joseph again held the keys, as once more Joseph was put in charge of all things in his world—because his new master, the keeper of the jail, found him to be trustworthy. God gave Joseph success in whatever he did.

Joseph's life was God centered, so nothing could throw him off balance. He served God first, and so he could then serve others.

Soon we meet the king's cupbearer and baker. They were put under Joseph's care in prison, and he attended them. He took a servant's role. He looked at them and paid attention to them. Joseph looked at them and asked, "Why are your faces so sad?" He took the time to listen to them and their stories of dreams they'd had, and then give them the wisdom he had, all in God's name.

How often do we go about our way and never even notice the people in our paths? How often do we look into the faces of the people God has placed around us? It seems a small thing to listen to someone's dream—certainly not life changing. But God uses small things to accomplish great purposes.[31] Listening to their two bizarre dreams—small things in the course of a day—would change not only Joseph's circumstances but also his entire life. And so much bigger than that, these same small dreams would change the history of nations.

For the time being, though, it appeared that Joseph's life wasn't going to change much, and the days continued to unfold as they had, one after another. Joseph served loyally and faithfully where God had placed him because his life was focused on God. And we leave Joseph still locked in the dungeon, falsely accused, unjustly imprisoned. The baker's dream was fulfilled as Joseph had said: he was hung. The cupbearer's dream was also fulfilled just as Joseph had interpreted: he was back at Pharaoh's side, serving wine and political advice.

Where was the justice? Joseph was innocent of wrongdoing, and God was with him—but he was still locked away, loyally serving, in prison.

A few years ago a young woman rear-ended me as I was waiting to merge into oncoming traffic. She was distraught over hitting me and very apologetic. I felt for her as we waited for the police to arrive. The officer gave her a ticket for failing to yield. Her insurance repaired my car. So I was surprised when I received a subpoena to appear in court over the accident. For four hours I listened to all the other cases that came before the judge. All of them, except for two, were declared guilty and fined—whether they pled guilty or not guilty. In almost every case the fines were too heavy to pay. The judge was smart and tough, and he did not suffer fools gladly. It was judgment, and everyone walking away from that bench was sad or angry.

I had whispered to the young woman that I was not there to testify against her, but *for* her. So she declared, "Not guilty, your honor."

When we were called to the bench, I was asked to testify first, which I did on her behalf. Then I asked the judge to be merciful to her, and he was: he totally dismissed the case. She was guilty—but she never even had to speak. I had stepped in for her. When the judge asked me if I was satisfied that the debt had been paid, I could honestly nod my head and say yes.

That is what we have in Jesus. We stand before God, our Judge, guilty and with no hope of justice, deserving a fine too heavy to pay, but Jesus speaks for us and asks for mercy.

The disciple Peter was there to watch Jesus, Son of God Most High, as He was crucified. Later Peter wrote to remind us that Jesus, who was without sin, submitted to insults and suffering, paying a price too heavy for us to pay because He had entrusted Himself to "him who judges justly" (1 Peter 2:23).

God stripped Joseph of his pride so he could become God centered instead of self-centered. No matter what his situation, Joseph served God with honor. He was trustworthy and loyal because he kept his eyes on God instead of circumstances.

God is just. God is with us. Do you trust Him when your world seems unfair and there appears to be no way out? Do you believe that God can use the most difficult times to build your character? Are you focused on *what* you can see ... or *who* you can trust?

If you are forgotten in a prison, helplessly watching one day fold into the next, lift your head. You are not alone there. Keep your eyes always on the Lord. He is there with you. He is at your right hand. You will not be shaken. Keep your eyes on Him.

28
EXTREME CHANGES
Read Genesis 41–44

After Joseph had been sold into slavery by his brothers and now languished in an Egyptian prison, his brothers were going merrily about their way in the land of Canaan, marrying and having children, apparently with their horrible sin against God and Joseph hidden neatly under the rug. Well, things were about to change—drastically.

Joseph would experience extreme changes in his position and power. The brothers, especially Judah, would experience extreme changes in their hearts and in humility. Joseph, a slave, would become a prince of Egypt. His brother Judah, who lived as something of a prince in his father's land, would offer to give up his own freedom and position to become a slave—ironically and unknowingly to his very own brother that he had sold into slavery.

It's a great story.

Almost every great story we have is based on this sort of turnaround. My personal favorite, *Cinderella*, runs along the same plot line. It starts with the evil stepmother and stepsisters who are so cruel to poor Cinderella, making her sleep near the ashes of the fireplace simply to keep warm. They take off for the ball, and suddenly Cinderella's fairy godmother shows up to magically change a pumpkin into a carriage and her rags into a gown. Off Cinderella goes to dance with the prince. No one recognizes her until later when the lost glass slipper magically fits her foot and her life changes forever.

Well, we may not have a fairy godmother and a magic wand to transform our lives, but our lives can be transformed just the same. Joseph saw this happen, and he completely understood it. He spoke very clearly the truth of the matter when he said: "God has made me fruitful in the land of my suffering" (Genesis 41:52).

God used experiences and dreams to change Joseph's position and power. The experiences were devastating while they were happening: God allowed Joseph to be sold into slavery and hauled off to a foreign land. Then He placed him in Potiphar's house, where he prospered and learned how to wisely manage an Egyptian household and fields. He was given the opportunity to develop important administrative skills. He was able to learn the language and the customs of Egypt. Because of the household where God placed him, Joseph was able to observe the politics of Pharaoh's court.

Then God allowed him to be falsely accused by Potiphar's wife, and suddenly Joseph became intimately aware of injustice—and compassion. He grew in wisdom instead of becoming bitter. He learned the hardship of waiting and the value of doing all things to the best of your ability—no matter the circumstances.

He learned to trust God when everything looked hopeless. And in God's hands, nothing is wasted. Even a prison became

Joseph's "networking opportunity," because God can use dreams to speak truth to us and lead us where He wants us to go.

God used dreams in Joseph's situation—and He still does, especially in cultures where freedom of speech is restricted and Christianity is illegal. God used three sets of dreams in Joseph's life. When he was a young man, he dreamed first of his brothers' sheaves of wheat bowing down to his own, and then he dreamed that the sun, moon, and the stars bowed down to him—representing his own family. These dreams certainly didn't make him popular with his family, but despite impossible circumstances, they would come true!

Then, while in prison, Joseph called on God to interpret the dreams of the cupbearer and the baker. Joseph predicted that one would be restored to his position of serving Pharaoh and one would be hanged, and these dreams came true.

Dreams. The veil of sleep lays heavy as our brains walk through the night without supervision. It is fascinating that God uses our dreams to speak to us.

So it was through Joseph's ability to understand the obscure meaning of dreams that Joseph found himself before Pharaoh. There, in very clear language, Joseph denied that he could interpret dreams—but, he said, God could!

Joseph spoke, and Pharaoh learned that his dream of seven sleek and fat cows being eaten by seven skinny, ugly cows meant that seven years of prosperity and bounty would be followed by seven years of famine. Pharaoh's second dream of wheat meant the same thing, Joseph said. Then God gave Joseph the wisdom to offer great advice—I love this! All those years in captivity prepared him for this next bold offer of how to approach coming hardship. Even Pharaoh of Egypt could plainly see the Spirit of God at work in the life of this Hebrew slave Joseph.

In the blink of an eye, Joseph the slave changed into Joseph the prince of Egypt. His power, privilege, and position all changed—because God made him fruitful in the land of his suffering.

Are you in a place of suffering? Are you allowing God to make you fruitful while you are there? Do you think He can use these hard circumstances to prepare you for something later in your life?

If you are in a difficult place of suffering, God is not surprised. He doesn't look down and say, "Well! How did you end up there?" He knows. He saw it coming. He carefully allowed it to happen. In His big scheme of things, something good can come from it. Stop being bewildered, hurt, or angry. Those are things that hold you captive in the miry pit of Satan's lies.

Instead, hold on to God's hand. Look Him in the face and say, "I trust You. Lead me into the light of Your love and mercy. Use me, Lord, for Your good. Make me bear fruit in the land of my suffering."

My sister Kathy died from ovarian cancer in 2007. At her memorial service, one person after another got up to speak about her wonderful personality, her character, and her bravery in facing her illness. They talked about her caring nature and how inspirational she was. My mother, my oldest sister, and I sort of looked at each other with an expression that said, "Are they talking about Kathy?"

She was our family, and we knew her in a way that her friends did not. We knew the very human flaws and struggles she battled against. Her friends watched her soar as she fought a deadly disease with one adamant conviction that she proclaimed over and over: "God is good. God is good. God is good." She was holding on tightly to God's hand and trusting Him to be good. Because of that, she conquered much and became a huge encouragement to the many people surrounding her. Not only that, I believe God revealed Himself and His Son Jesus to her in her dreams. My sister Kathy, who hated the name of Jesus, came to know Him as her Savior during the last weeks of her life. God made her fruitful in the land of her suffering.

Life experience and dreams changed Joseph too. It was an extreme changeover in his position and power, and God made him fruitful in the land of his suffering.

The famine Joseph prophesied by way of dream interpretation finally came, and it was indeed extreme. It reached beyond the boundaries of Egypt and into the land of Canaan, affecting the lives of Joseph's brothers and father. So the boys trotted off to Egypt, silver in hand, to buy life-giving grain. In that distant land was food that existed only because God could change evil, self-centered intentions into good.

Think about it! God used the brother they'd sold into slavery to interpret Pharaoh's dreams and prepare seven years in advance for an upcoming worldwide famine! This was huge! Can you imagine the power of weather forecasters if they could do that today?

Ironically the brothers had no idea who they were approaching. Joseph had no idea what kind of men they were now—he only knew who they were the last time he had seen them. So he devised four tests—tests to determine their character and to reveal their hearts.

First, he accused them of being spies and then threw them into prison for a few days. Vengeful? Not exactly: Joseph was looking for remorse. Did they regret what they'd done to him? I wonder if they were in the same prison where Joseph had been for so many years? As they told their story to him and talked among themselves, Joseph could see true sorrow for what they'd done to him. They knew well that what they had done was wrong in the eyes of God.

Then came the second test: Joseph sent them on their way home, holding Simeon captive until they could return with Benjamin, the youngest brother. But Joseph also returned their silver in the sacks with the grain they'd just purchased. How honest were they? What was their integrity like? They would return for Simeon with brother Benjamin in tow, and they would also bring back the hidden silver along with additional gifts. Can you imagine how long that trip felt to them? They were walking back and forth on the same path they had sent Joseph on all those many years ago—a broken young man, his heart filled with sorrow, alone.

The third test: Joseph invited them to lunch at his house. A little chicken salad, cucumber sandwiches, and petit fours, and he gave youngest son, Benjamin, Daddy's new favorite, five times as much as he gave anyone else. No one seemed to bat an eye. They no longer seemed to be vengeful or jealous when one brother was shown favoritism over another.

Then there was the fourth and final test. Joseph's favorite silver cup "mysteriously" ended up in baby boy Benjamin's sack. Now was the elder brothers' chance to ditch this favorite younger brother, and it would be by no fault of their own. They could easily return and show up at Israel's door without Benjamin: "Too bad, so sad. That crazy Egyptian fellow kept him. Caught him stealing in fact, and we couldn't do a thing about it. Wasn't our fault. Sorry."

But that was not the way the story ended because God had done a mighty change in the hearts of these brothers. Their hearts were now filled with humility, and their hearts were broken at the horrific thought of losing another brother.

We see Judah, clothes torn in mourning, down on the ground before this Egyptian accuser and judge begging for mercy: "What can we say? What can we say? How can we prove our innocence? God has uncovered our guilt! We are now all your slaves" (44:18–34, my brief paraphrase).

This is miraculous! This is Judah, the one who suggested they sell their brother into slavery. This is Judah, who held back his third son from Tamar. This is Judah, who unknowingly slept with his own daughter-in-law, thinking she was a temple prostitute. This is Judah, who suddenly stepped up to take full responsibility for the life of another when he could have just as easily walked away.

God had changed his heart, and it was evident in his actions. One man, Judah, offered his life for another. Though he was not guilty of the crime—and the younger, favorite brother Benjamin appeared to be the "innocent" brother—Judah was laying down his life as a substitute to take the punishment for another man's sin. "I cannot return to my father without him," Judah explained to Joseph. "My father's life is closely bound up with this boy's life. How can I go back to my father if he is not with me?" (vv. 31, 34, my paraphrase). Judah offered his life for another's.

Isn't that the story of another Son—the Son named Jesus? "I have come to give you life," He said. "I am the good Shepherd who lays down His life for His sheep" (John 10:10–11, my paraphrase). Jesus entered a "foreign" land and offered His life in exchange for the lives of the accused, those found guilty of sin against the King. "How can I go back to my Father if this man or this woman is not with Me?" He came to give His life for ours so that we could return to our Father, who waits for our return. Our Father *waits for our return.*

And because of that, everything changes.

If you stand accused, there is One who offers to lay down His life for you. If you are held captive in the land of sorrow, there is One who can free you. Can you let go of your anger and resentment? Can you accept God's forgiveness? And standing forgiven, can you forgive others?

Will hard circumstances make you bitter or make you better? Are you willing to be changed? There is a Brother who was willing to give up His life for you. He stands before the Judge. He takes your guilt onto His shoulders and will bear your shame. He made a promise that He would not return home without you. Your Father is waiting for your return. Take hold of your Brother's hand. He will lead you safely home.

29
... BUT GOD
Read Genesis 45–46

Do you believe God is sovereign? Those of us who have been around Christian circles for a while will immediately answer, "Yes, of course, God is Supreme Ruler over all things." The story of Joseph is a perfect example of God's sovereignty.

He was sold into slavery by his mean brothers only to be catapulted from servant to prisoner to second in charge of all of Egypt, simply by some creative dream interpretation, and now he was standing with his brothers' lives literally in his hands. Well, the only way you can explain that is "God is sovereign." The word "sovereign" means "one who exercises supreme, permanent authority."[32] God has power over all things. We say that, but believing it in our heart of hearts when the bad guys have just stripped us naked and smeared blood on our favorite coat is a lot harder thing to do.

What do you think of this quote: "We don't see things as *they* are, we see things as *we* are"?[33] Our view is limited. We can only see what is in the room with us. We don't see the much bigger picture of what is going on outside the room.

Years ago I watched news footage shot from a helicopter of a tsunami in Japan as it was taking place. There were horrible images of that wave of water and trash rolling forward, destroying everything in its path: houses, buildings, fields. Looking down on it from above, you could see a road running parallel to the oncoming water, and slowly you realized that there was a tiny white car driving along that road, trying to get away. Its way was blocked, so it turned around. From our view above we could see the wall of water coming, but I am sure, as they traveled along that road, they couldn't possibly see how vast the wave was that rolled toward them. The helicopter continued flying its path deeper inland, away from the oncoming tide, and I don't know what happened to that little white car and the people inside.

Simply "seeing" from above is not enough. If we believe God sees from above yet is powerless to act, then that does little good at all. Why would you care about a God who doesn't interact with you? Of what purpose is a God if He has no power? I love what Joseph told his brothers: "It was not you who sent me here, but God."

Joseph knew. Joseph totally understood that God did more than simply watch from above. He knew that God got involved. God rolled up His sleeves and acted. God was not watching quietly from a distance while Joseph's brothers sent him off to Egypt naked and bound. Joseph said, "So then, it was not you who sent me here, but God ..." (Genesis 45:8). Look at the way it is written: a comma, then "but God."

Joseph was saying, "From my perspective, something terrible seemed to be happening <comma> *BUT GOD* ... But God was in control. But God was taking me where He wanted me to go. But God was changing my path. But God was separating me from those people and connecting me to others. But God was teaching me compassion and wisdom. But God was changing history in a profound way. So it was not you who sent me here, but God."

It was God who could see all the way from Canaan to Egypt. It was God who could see the past and the promises He had made to Abraham. It was God who could see into the future and knew a famine would bring Abraham's descendants into Egypt for a time. "It was not you who sent me here, *but God*," Joseph said.

If anyone of Joseph's generation could remember God's little chat with Great-Grandfather Abraham, they would recall Him telling of an upcoming time of captivity for these children to come: "Then the LORD said to Abram, 'You can be sure that your descendants will be strangers in a foreign land, where they will be oppressed as slaves for 400 years'" (15:13 NLT). Even if they could recall this prophecy, I am willing to bet that they couldn't see the big picture at the moment—they were too close to what was unfolding in their small lives.

There are three stories here: Joseph's story, the brothers' story, and Jacob's story. From a human perspective, it looked like something tragic and dark was happening, but God, from His perspective, was doing something wonderful and far-reaching.

Let's start with Joseph's story. Joseph's brothers were before him, and we hear him tell them, "I am your brother Joseph that you sold into Egypt." What we forget, because we are reading everything in English, is that Joseph, all decked out in his Egyptian attire, had been speaking in the Egyptian language through an interpreter up this point. Suddenly he began weeping so loud that the neighbors could hear him—and then he started speaking to them in their native Hebrew tongue.

Can you imagine what a shock this was? It completely freaked them out!

Joseph gave them beautiful, loving descriptions of what was really happening: "You sold me into Egypt, but God sent me ahead of you to prepare a place and to save your lives. You sold me into Egypt, but God made me the father to Pharaoh, giving me a position of power and authority over the royal ruler. You sold me into Egypt, but God made me Lord over Pharaoh's household and all of Egypt. It was not you who sent me here, but God" (45:4–8, my paraphrase).

Joseph and his brothers could not possibly see that God was doing something even bigger than that. Joseph's life, in many ways, pointed to the life of Jesus, who was yet to come. Both were beloved sons of their fathers. Both were sent to their brothers with a message. Both were rejected by their brothers: Joseph was thrown into a pit; Jesus was beaten and crucified. Both were sold for silver. Both were sent to a distant place: Joseph went to Egypt; Jesus ascended to heaven. Both were delivered from undeserved suffering and raised to positions of authority: Joseph to Pharaoh's right hand; Jesus to God's right hand. Both acquired a bride with pagan connections: Joseph's bride was the daughter of an Egyptian priest; Jesus's Bride is the church, which has been predominately Gentile for the last two thousand years. And Joseph, mourned by his family as dead, like Jesus, suddenly was in their presence, symbolically raised from the dead.[34]

Who could possibly conceive this, *but God*?

The brothers had their own story. From their point of view, they had been living a decent life providing for their families and honoring their father. Except for a couple of unfortunate events along the way, they had been upstanding men. Then a famine threatened their very lives. They heard that Egypt had grain. So off they went, hoping to get enough food to survive until the rains came again.

Survival—that's all they were hoping for. But God instead gave them their long-lost brother, reuniting their family with no anger or bitterness. God gave them reconciliation. They went for grain, but God gave them favor in a foreign king's eyes. Not only were they not condemned or enslaved, but they were welcomed by Pharaoh himself. They were given royal favor, protection from harm. They went for grain, but God gave them material blessings beyond their wildest dreams: carts, clothing, money, food, and livestock. He gave them not only material necessities but also bountiful provision with all the extra frills.

They went for grain, but God gave them a new home. Joseph told them, "You shall live in the region of Goshen and be near me—you, your children and grandchildren, your flocks and herds, and all you have" (v. 10). Land: a place to raise their families and their livestock, a place to live and grow and prosper. They went for grain, and Joseph threw his arms around them and wept and kissed them and gave them forgiveness.

As Jesus said, "Ask and it will be given to you; seek and you will find; knock and the door will be opened to you. ... If you, then, though you are evil, know how to give good gifts to your children, how much more will your Father in heaven give good gifts to those who ask him!" (Matthew 7:7, 11). Undeserving, we ask for grain, but God desires to give us greater gifts. What a great picture of the generosity of God!

The brothers returned to Jacob with stories of forgiveness, and Jacob saw the miraculous provisions sent to convince him of his living son. This would be much like what Jacob's descendants many years later would experience. Jesus brought them stories of forgiveness and performed miracles of provision. Water would be turned into wine. Bread would multiply to feed thousands. All of this would be to convince the unbelieving observers of a living Son—a Son who offered forgiveness.

This is where we meet up with Jacob's story again. His struggles in life had produced a ragtag bunch of sons: brothers born from four different mothers. Remember all the messes we have been through with Jacob? He was much less the hero than we want him to be in his role of Father Israel. But God called each of Jacob's sons by name. Twelve sons would become twelve tribes. These twelve tribes would form the nation of Israel, from which a king named David would come. And a Savior named Jesus would come out of the tribe of Judah. Judah: the brother who was willing to lay his life down for his brother Benjamin.

All of them would be set apart for a while in the land of Egypt through their brother Joseph's provision. Even the years ahead, which would become a time of slavery, would be for their protection. They would be set apart, separate from the people they were living among so that they could grow into the people who would become known as God's chosen.

"It was not you who sent me here, but God."

When you really think about this statement, it's outrageous! Those two little words "but God" become two of the most powerful words I have ever thought about. I know it is easy to say, "God is sovereign," yet it is hard to think that He has put us or allowed us to remain in the middle of a mess for some better purpose.

Take this verse, "It was not _____ who sent me here, but God," and use it as a fill-in-the-blank to apply to your own life. What is the hard place, the most devastating experience, the most hurtful person in your life? Put it in the blank. For Joseph, it was "my brothers." For you, it may be a friend who betrayed your trust or a spouse who cheated on you. Or a parent who abandoned you, or a boss who belittled you publicly, or a teacher who wrote you off, or a child who has rebelled and broken your heart. We all have those hurts that we can't see beyond, but God can.

Can you trust that He will use this for good? Do you believe that God is actively involved in your life? Will you rest in Him, knowing that there is a bigger story unfolding? It is the story of a God who prepares a banquet when we are desperate for a piece of bread. It is the story of a God who can lead us into a dark prison to prepare us to lead a nation into the light. The world may seem a hard and hopeless place, but God goes before you preparing the way into life. Go with Him. He knows the bigger picture. You can trust Him. Our God is sovereign.

30
JACOB'S STORY: A PILGRIM IN A FOREIGN LAND
Read Genesis 47–48

I am a pilgrim and a stranger
Traveling through this wearisome land
And I've got a home in that yonder city, good Lord
And it's not (good Lordy it's not) not made by hand

—"The Wayfaring Pilgrim" song[35]

My name is Israel. Some call me Jacob. You may not think you know me, but you do—you know me very well actually.

My father was Isaac. The Isaac that Abraham bound with ropes and laid on a distant altar to sacrifice as a burnt offering to his God, the One he called "Sovereign Lord." God asked Grandfather Abraham to do this unbelievable thing—to plunge a knife into his long-awaited son Isaac—but fortunately for my dad (and for me!), God stopped his upraised hand at the last second and provided a ram for the sacrifice instead. But it was a close one. And it made quite an impression, I tell you.

You see, Grandfather Abraham and this God who spoke to him face-to-face had made vows to each other. God had a plan to bless Abraham with land as far as he could see and descendants too many to count. Those descendants would become their own nation—actually many nations—with rulers and royal kings. Others we met who blessed us would be blessed, while those who cursed us would be cursed. We would have a huge impact on all peoples of the earth: we would be a blessing to them. As a sign of this covenant, we would be circumcised—a powerful reminder right there on the tip of our manhood. It would help us to remember—night and day—that we were God's people and He was our God.

Grandfather Abraham and God went to a lot of trouble to find the perfect wife for my daddy, Isaac. They sent back to the old country for her among our relatives so that she would have common values and upbringing and would worship our God. Her name was Rebekah. Young and beautiful, she was also confident and hardworking and maybe a little strong-willed. Daddy fell in love with her the moment he saw her coming across the fields to become his bride.

My mom, Rebekah, loved to tell me the story of how when she was pregnant, there was such a commotion within her swelling belly that she called out to God, "What is going on? Why is this happening? I feel as if this baby is going to push right through my skin!"

God told her, "There is not one baby, but two! They will become two separate nations. One nation will be stronger than the other—and the oldest son will serve the youngest."

Well, my brother Esau came out first, so he was the oldest. But I came out right behind him, holding firmly to his heel. My mother would laugh as she told me this story because she certainly saw it in me: this competitiveness. I didn't want to be second best or left behind in anything—competitive from birth, I always wanted to be first.

I was really close to my mother. Esau was close to our dad. It's just the way it was. My brother, Esau, and I really didn't have anything in common. Esau loved to be outside, roaming the hills hunting for wild game. I liked more disciplined pursuits—I enjoyed farming and caring for the herds, and my mom taught me to become a great cook.

Esau was so overly dramatic and just lived for the moment. He loved to act helpless when it came to taking care of himself. He came in one day from hunting, collapsing in the doorway. "I am just famished!" he said. "I will die if I don't eat this moment!"

Please! I thought. *If you are going to act the fool and die from "spontaneous hunger," I am going to call your bluff.*

So I said, "Sell me your birthright, O firstborn—your inheritance for a bowl of stew."

I thought he would never be so stupid to agree—but he did! How ridiculous! To give up everything for nothing. But that was Esau, not realizing or appreciating the honors he had, only wishing for what he didn't have at that moment. He sold his birthright, the privilege of being the oldest son, for a silly bowl of tomato soup!

Well, in our culture, your word is golden, so once said, it was done. He gave me, with the nod of his head, the honor and privilege of the oldest son.

For my part—and my dear mother's—I am embarrassed to tell you what happened next, but you already know it, don't you? The stealing of my brother's blessing from our own father.

After my mother overheard my father tell Esau he wanted to give him his blessing, Mom and I kicked into overdrive to make sure I got there first. My mother brought me my brother's clothes so I would smell like the outdoors—like him. She cooked Dad's favorite stew while I covered my arms and the back of my neck with the skins from the goats I had just killed for the stew. You see, Dad couldn't see very well anymore—so we were counting on him thinking I was Esau with his hairy arms and outdoor smells.

I know, I know. You are thinking, *How could you and your mother do such a thing?* It was just that my mother knew Isaac was supposed to bless me above Esau—and she just thought God needed a little help to make that happen.

> So I lied
> and deceived,
> my own father—
> and broke my brother's heart in the process.
> Because I was selfish
> and thought I had to make things happen
> my way.

My brother's anger rained down on me—so much so that he wished me dead. But my dear mother figured out a way to protect me for a while. With my father's permission, she sent me back to the old country to her brother Laban, to find a suitable wife. I left, not knowing I would never see her again.

So began my journey through life as a pilgrim: alone, with no possessions, no wealth, and little provisions, leaving behind a shattered family. The only things I possessed were my brother's birthright, a stolen blessing for my future, and a bad reputation as a deceiver.

But something happened one night when I was alone out there in the desert under the stars: I dreamed a dream.

You know about this also. It is such an interesting, fascinating idea that three thousand years later men still write songs about it: "Stairway to Heaven." Well, it was amazing to see—this stairway with its bottom resting on earth and its top reaching to heaven with angels of God ascending and descending on it. There at the top stood the Lord—and He spoke to me.

He promised the land I was lying on.

He promised descendants as numerous as the dust of the earth.

He said all peoples on earth would be blessed through me—and my children's children.

But He also said something I could hold onto. Before the land would come, or the children, or the blessings to people in some future time, He said, "I am with you and will watch over you wherever you go, and I will bring you back to this land. I am with you" (Genesis 28:15, my paraphrase).

A pilgrim, yes. Traveling to God knows where. But I would no longer be alone ... because my God was with me, watching over me, wherever I would go.

That changed everything for me.

God was taking me into a new land—where He would grow me up. I fell in love with Rachel, daughter of my mother's brother Laban. But just as I had deceived my father, Laban deceived me. For, after working seven years for Rachel's dowry, I was given her older sister Leah instead! To make up for that, Laban also gave me Rachel as a wife—for another seven years of labor. Thus began a mess of two wives and jealousy, and throw in two of their servants to fuel the competitive baby race, and I found myself years down the road with eleven sons, a daughter, and four wives—and still working for my father-in-law with no land of my own.

God came to me again and said: "Go back to the land of your fathers and I will be with you" (31:3, my paraphrase).

So off we went: out of the frying pan of my father-in-law Laban and into the fire of facing my angry brother, Esau.

I was terrified, fearing the loss of everything I loved, but God Himself came to me at night in the form of an angel—and wrestled with me. It sounds crazy, I know, but I am a wrestling kind of man, so that is how God came to me. I was born wrestling, struggling, with my twin, Esau, and then as an adult with Laban. But God wanted me to understand that my struggle, my wrestling, was with Him. No matter how hard I pushed back, I had to submit to Him. He was the one who controlled my destiny—not me, with all my manipulations and cunning. He changed my name from Jacob to Israel that night because my struggles would not end—but I would overcome my struggles. I made my peace with God.

I also made my peace with Esau, and we went on to settle the land one place and then another. Family tragedies took place along the way, breaking my heart and bending my head in sorrow. If you were to look at me from the safety of your church pew, you might wonder what happened to this old fearful, self-centered man. But what you forget is that God still appeared to me at night: He called my name, and I answered, "Here I am."

God set my life into motion again: "Do not be afraid to go down to Egypt. I will go with you, and I will surely bring you back again" (46:4, my paraphrase).

So off I went again to a foreign land—knowing I am never alone, but that God goes with me. Knowing that I can travel with my eleven sons to the son who waited for us, where they will become the twelve tribes of Israel and will produce descendants as numerous as the dust of the desert—these sons of mine who caused great hurt and harm to me and to each other. But God was with me.

We would travel through lands bleak and dry with famine and into a foreign land of strangers. My son Joseph waited for us with the best land for our livestock and the protection and favor of Pharaoh himself. There would be grain to fill our bellies and grain to plant for the coming years.

God was with me, so I could stand taller than Pharaoh of Egypt and bless *him*.

God was with me, so I knew the future would unfold under the protection of God's hand. I had been a pilgrim, but God was my Shepherd leading me where He would have me go. He was the angel who not only wrestled me but also delivered me from all harm. When I thought my son Joseph dead, God knew he was in Egypt preparing a place for us.

So there I was, Israel, an old man, going into a strange land: Egypt.

What did I leave behind? What did I have to show for my life of wrestling with God and everyone else? What happened to God's promise of land?

There I was with sons and grandchildren, yet I could not see the generations to come or how those boys of mine could possibly touch all the peoples on earth as God had promised for so long.

What would I do with those unfulfilled promises of God? Would I trust Him no longer?

Far be it from me! I would yet worship Him and call upon His name. He had been my constant Shepherd. He delivered me from harm along the way. Every step along my pilgrim's journey, I was never alone, for my God was with me!

31
LAVISH BLESSINGS
Read Genesis 49:1–28

Years ago our family would awake early on the first Sunday in May and take our annual journey to Alabama—to the tiny community of Wadley. We traveled deep into the country-side—most of the community was made up of woods and fields with houses scattered here and there down long dirt driveways. Our destination was a little redbrick church—the kind with one center aisle and open windows and doors because there was no air-conditioning. Along with the assorted hymnals in the wooden pews, we would find old-fashioned cardboard paddle fans with beautiful vistas painted on them, or Jesus holding a lamb, or the most current editions that had advertisements for men running for local government offices, which I found a little strange. But I digress ...

The event that drew us there was the yearly homecoming at Forester Chapel, the tiny church in the farming community where my husband, Jeff's, mother had grown up. "First Sunday in May" was my mother-in-law's favorite day of the year, as every-one who still had breath in them gathered for the church service, lunch (or "dinner," as it is called in the South) on the grounds afterward, and a mandatory stroll through the graveyard to look at all the flowers that families had placed on the graves.

On a typical journey to the church, we passed what was left of the wooden house where my mother-in-law Nell had lived with her family of twelve: her beloved parents, her two brothers, and most importantly her seven sisters. Once vibrant with daily living and many voices in the 1920s, '30s, and even '40s, it was barely standing—an empty shell of weather-worn wood, the remnant of a porch, and a roof long since fallen in.

But at the end of the road, we arrived at our destination: Forester Chapel. Dust kicked up in the red-clay parking lot of the little church. There were plenty of cars, and a long row of concrete tables spread out across the back under the oak trees was set up for the shared community potluck dinner afterward. On First Sunday in May, the church was so packed that people hung around outside the door, coming and going, leaning in to see if there was an available seat or if their loved ones were already inside or if this was the part of the program they wanted to hear. Now the preaching at First Sunday often was the "hellfire and damnation" kind—with lots of yelling and crying going on—or it could be the soft-spoken rambling of the "God is love and forgiveness" kind. You never knew what you were going to get—but the music was always Southern gospel in four-part harmony. And that was the best part.

They sang before the preaching and after, but the part you couldn't miss happened after dinner when we all came back into the church with bellies full and listened to various groups sing their favorite hymns. Jeff's multitude of cousins sang in different gospel groups, and in between their turn up front when they sang their favorite songs, they would tell stories of growing up, sitting between their mother and their father, learning all the different parts of the harmony for each song.

Jeff's mother was Nellie Gray—one of the famous (in those parts) Gray Girls. There were eight girls in the Gray family, and different combinations of them sang at different times through the years (their papa had taught them over five hundred songs). But Jeff's mother, Nellie, with her beautiful, steady alto, was always one of the favorites.

On the very last First Sunday in May that we attended, an hour or so into the gospel singing, Jeff and his brother, Burt, were recognized. People applauded and strained in their seats to turn and look at them and acknowledge them with a smile. When it was all over, many people came up to tell them stories of what they remembered about Jeff and Burt's mother. Now Jeff and Burt don't sing, but because their mother did—and was so well known and thought of—they inherited the praise and reputation of the Gray family name and heritage.

Who we are is bigger than who *we are* individually. We inherit gifts, traits, characteristics, and reputations all tangled up in the family we came from—and those inherited qualities become a bigger picture of who we are. The people who came before us pour out their blessings onto those of us who come after.

This story from Genesis 49 is the telling of family tales. These are the people God chose to call his family. He told Abraham: "You will be My people and I will be your God" (Genesis 17:7, my paraphrase).

So we follow their genealogy from Adam to Noah to Abraham to Jacob—and we learn the family stories of their adventures and misadventures. Sometimes we are proud to stand up and be acknowledged, and other times we just wish all the neighbors didn't know our business, as my aunt Doris used to say.

This is a story of blessings from fathers. It is a family story of Father Abraham to Jacob and Joseph—but it is much more than that. It is the story of Father God, who loved the world so much that *He gave His own Son* ... so that we might understand what being His child looks like—and through that understanding might *become* His children, adopted into His family. Adopted by God, we share in the privileges, the responsibilities, the blessings of being His own.

The blessings of our Father on His children are lavish. I love that word—that thought: "lavish blessings."

> "How great is *the love* the Father has lavished on
> us, that we should be called children of God"
> (1 John 3:1, my paraphrase).

This story of Israel has been a story of blessings from the Father. It is one specific family's story, but it is so much more than that. The blessings from God to Abraham, to Isaac, to Jacob who became Israel, would now flow into these twelve sons of Israel. These twelve sons will become twelve tribes who will become the nation of Israel, and they will spread God's blessings from one chosen people to the very ends of the earth. But today we gather in the room with the family to hear the last words of Israel.

The blessings we hear from the voice of Israel make us pause. We hear the grievous sins of Reuben, Simeon, and Levi spoken out loud for all to hear, and we cringe. How could they have made these horrible choices that caused such harm? Were they still unrepentant, justifying their actions, glossing over their violence and holding tightly to their pride? Each son was called by name, and a blessing that rested on the past and looked forward to the future was placed upon his head.

This scene in the bedchambers of Israel is an uncomfortable reminder for us that another time is approaching when we all will stand before our Father and His hand will lay heavy on our heads. Will His assessment of our lives unfold as an irrefutable damnation, or will we receive the reward of His blessing? Will we be sent outside the gates of the family with wailing and gnashing of teeth? Or will we be called "faithful child of God" and receive the lavish love of our Father?

But for now, let's lean into the blessings of Israel on two of his sons: Judah and Joseph. These two sons received the longest and most hope-filled blessings. Judah, the fourth son of Israel, was born of the unloved bride, Leah. Joseph, the lost yet favored younger son, was born of the cherished wife, Rachel. We have traveled the road with these two brothers, and we think we can see where all this is headed. Joseph would continue in wealth and power, and his descendants would be immersed in God's blessings. Joseph was called a prince among his brothers. We think to ourselves that Joseph would continue to be this favored son who would carry forth the story. We think it will be Joseph who will have a royal son come from his line—a King, a Savior, right?

Not quite.

Surprisingly, when we dig down and read between the lines in the blessing of Judah, it is there we find the blessings of a King to come:

"Your hand will be on the neck of your enemies; your father's sons will bow down to you" (Genesis 49:8). "You are a lion—who will dare to disturb you? You will carry a scepter and a ruler's staff" (vv. 9–10, my paraphrase).

These are the instruments of a king. It would be from Judah that a king named David would rise to the throne. He would be the greatest king of the nation of Israel, and his descendant would be a man named Jesus who would enter Jerusalem amid shouts of "Hosanna to the Son of David!" A King arrived who would save His people. A King who was the descendant of both David and Judah. The scepter had come to whom it belonged.

We must look at more of the blessing Judah received:

"He will [tether] his donkey to a vine, his colt to the choicest branch; he will wash his garments in wine, his robes in the blood of grapes" (v. 11, my paraphrase).

Judah's descendant Jesus would arrive in Israel's Holy City on the colt of a donkey proclaiming to be the "choicest branch." As Jesus said, "I am the true vine, and my Father is the gardener" (John 15:1). A few days later, during His last meal, this unlikely King would symbolically wash his garments in the blood of grapes when He offered His raised Passover cup of wine as His own blood. Within hours He would wear a kingly crown of thorns, and a royal purple robe would be placed over His shoulders as He was mocked and struck in the face. He would be beaten and His blood would stain the streets of His holy city. The sign that would hang over His head as He bled on a Roman cross would declare to the world His crime of being

"King of the Jews." He would tell those who would listen that He had come to lay down His life as a ransom for many.

We remember the story of Judah when he appeared before the Egyptian official (Joseph) and "laid down his life" for his brother Benjamin—offering to take his place and to receive the punishment for a crime he had not committed because he said that he could not return to his father without him. Judah had begged to give up his own life for his brother.

Jesus came to do the same. It was no accident that the family of Judah would carry the ultimate blessings. From the tribe of Judah would come God's chosen Messiah who would lay down His life for His people. Judah's descendant, who wore a crown, would be Jesus.

We can travel from Genesis, the book of beginnings, to the future portrayed in Revelation to read about the last days: there in the heavenly courts, where the Lion of the tribe of Judah will triumph. He will appear as the Lamb that was slain, standing in the center of the throne room. All will bow before Him and sing a new song:

> "You are worthy to take the scroll
> and to open its seals,
> because you were slain,
> and with your blood you purchased for God
> persons from every tribe and language and people
>   and nation.
> You have made them to be a kingdom and priests to
>   serve our God,
> and they will reign on the earth."
>   (Revelation 5:9–10)

This is the lavish blessing of the Father on the family of Judah: a royal King Messiah to rule for eternity. Lavish blessings of the Father!

But what about Joseph? What brought him into such a powerful role in this story of Israel and his twelve sons? What in the world, in the bigger scheme of things, was his purpose?

We can find it in his blessing.

The father's blessings upon Joseph were blessings of *provision* when all seemed impossible. Under God's watchful eye Joseph would become "a fruitful vine whose branches climb over a wall" (Genesis 49:22, my paraphrase).

Joseph was a savior to his family in Egypt, similar to how Jesus would become a Savior to those who were under enemy rule in Israel, with no hope and only death awaiting them. God provided this savior named Joseph just as God would provide a Savior named Jesus. We can't help but see the parallel between Joseph and Jesus, as we already looked at earlier. God Himself provided Joseph to save his brothers—as well as all the people who would come to him from Egypt and beyond. God provided Jesus to save Israel's descendants—as well as all the people in the world if we will come to Him.

"Through the blood of his Son, we are set free from our sins. God forgives our failures because of his overflowing kindness" (Ephesians 1:7 GWT). Lavish blessings from the Father—on Judah, on Joseph, on us!

Both Judah and Joseph traveled a twisting road. Their actions didn't always match up with the desires of their father. Yet God embraced them and watched over them and had amazing plans for their lives—plans that would affect generations of their descendants to come.

God has room for you in His family. He stands, with open arms, waiting for you to enter His chambers. Our Father God is a lavish giver of blessings, and He longs to lay His hand upon you and call you "My child."

Will you accept that invitation? Will you leave your old life and enter His family? Will you be adopted by God, to share in the privileges, the responsibilities, the blessings of being His own?

32
HEADING HOME
Read Genesis 49:29–33; 50

I have stories to tell of death and dying. I am grateful that I have been allowed to have deathbed conversations with those I have loved. Nothing left unsaid. Holding the hand of my sister or father or mother, looking into their eyes, lifting the cup of water to their lips, praying over them, counting the seconds as they took their last breath.

My sister, Kathy, who lived in Florida, decided three weeks before she passed away that she wanted to be buried in a "green burial" preserve. There would be no embalming. No waterproof metal casket. She would be buried under a sourwood tree along a wooded path that led down to a stream covered with mountain laurel—in South Carolina. I didn't know if it could be done. One of the hospice nurses argued with me adamantly that it would be against the law to fly her unembalmed body from Tampa to Greenville. But a week later our family gathered by her grave on a hillside in the woods near Ramsey Creek, reading from the book of Psalms in both Hebrew and English. Her body lay in a wooden casket, built with wooden pegs, covered with the petals of roses. We spoke of her life. Our nephew played "In the Garden" on his guitar, and we sang along. Then we covered the casket with earth until the entire grave was covered. Lastly, we planted native ferns over the mound, watered with the water from the creek. It was extremely private and personal, and we had honored her last wishes to take her home to South Carolina.

We are now at the end of this book of beginnings: Genesis. It comes to an end with the deaths of Jacob and Joseph. They have traveled long, on paths they could have never foreseen. Surrounded by family, they close their eyes for the last time, in a foreign land. They both have one last request: "Carry my bones out of this place, and take me home."

Home. Where was that?

For these Hebrew men, home was the land where their fathers had pitched their tents. It was the land where their fathers and mothers were buried. It was a purchased cave beside a field. It was a place they could point to that held the memories of what had gone before. Yet it wasn't the place as much as it was the people. The people who defined who they were. The people who knew them and cared about them. Home was where they were known by name. Home was where they had identity and presence, even when they were no longer there. Home.

We are reminded of the value of life in the ceremonies of death. In Jacob's death, we see the great sorrow of his son Joseph. He threw himself onto his father's lifeless body, weeping. There was a forty-day process of embalming his body—our sad human effort to undo or at least postpone the destruction of death. There was the royal procession to the place of burial, carrying all the weight of dignity and honor they could bestow.

And there were several more days—seven—of mourning and lamenting, causing the neighbors to take notice and give honor.

This is the problem, my friends: Death is not what God intended for His creation. He created us to live. He created us to love. He created us for joy and pleasure in the goodness of His creation. Our sin took all of that away from us. We turned our backs. The created turned their backs on the Creator, and death entered in. With death came mourning. We are painfully reminded of what we have forfeited, what we have given up when we turn away from our Creator.

But God, the Creator, could not leave us in the darkness of death. There were whispers of a rescue underway. God Himself would come to us. God Himself would defeat the hold that our sin and our death had on us. Some of us would cling to our own plans, refusing help, refusing the plans of our Creator—denying the power death had over us. But some would listen. Some would hear the life-giving words. Some would accept the offer of rescue. Some would cling to the hand of God and hear His words when He offered abundant life and told of a place of eternal life where each person would be known by name. This place would be called by many names: heaven, paradise, God's kingdom, "My Father's house," home.

My mother's last afternoon with me was very ordinary but very precious. She and I had run errands: getting manicures, laughing as we rode through a self-serve car wash, stopping for ice cream cones. That Saturday afternoon, as I prepared supper, she told me stories of her brothers getting up at four to milk the cows on their dairy farm, then bottling the milk and delivering it while her mother killed and plucked and fried the chickens and fixed the gravy and biscuits that would be their breakfast when they returned from their morning's work.

I settled her in the backyard at the picnic table, and then I went back inside to get our drinks. Three minutes later I returned to find her unconscious where she had fallen after hitting her head on a large terracotta planter. She regained consciousness, and I realized she'd had a stroke. But we talked for a few minutes as I assessed the damage and my husband called for an ambulance. I held her head tightly between my hands, looking into her gray eyes as I tried to stop the blood flow from the gash above her ear. Suddenly she stopped looking at me and responding to me.

Instead, she began crying out: "I want to go home, I want to go home."

I knew she was speaking of a *different home.*

She saw something very different beyond my suburban backyard. She wanted to go there. It was a home she had been waiting for. It was a home she recognized. These were the last words she said to me: "I want to go home."

"In My Father's house are many rooms;
if it were not so,
I would have told you.
I am going there
to prepare a place for you."
(John 14:2, my paraphrase)

My mother wanted to go home.

Jacob wanted to go home to be buried. Joseph wanted to make sure his final resting place would not be Egypt, but home. Why did it matter? If this brief moment we are alive is all that matters, why do we go through all these elaborate preparations and care of our physical bodies after the heart has stopped beating and the breath is gone? Why do we still embalm today, just as the Egyptians did so long ago? Why do we care where our bones rest? Why do we purchase watertight crypts and engrave granite tombstones?

Because in our heart of hearts, we *know*.
We know there is more than this—
much more—
and we don't want to miss it!
Because somehow we *know*
what comes after this
is more important than *this*—
and we want to be there.

God's blessing to Jacob, who became Israel, and then to Joseph many years later was a promised piece of land. It looked like an ordinary little cave beside a field bought from the Hittites, but it would become the center of the world. Not only for them but for the rest of the earth. The cave of Machpelah, purchased some 3,700 years ago by Abraham, would become home—the final resting place for Abraham, Isaac, Jacob, Sarah, Rebekah, and Leah: all of these Hebrew people that we have come to know so well.[36]

But "home" on this earth is hard to hold onto. That precious piece of land, Machpelah, was conquered seven hundred years ago and a mosque was built over those graves. For the Jews, access to the final resting place of their Hebrew ancestors is greatly restricted. Of all the land in this great big world, it is interesting that this tiny piece of it would become holy land—and tied to the hearts of three different people: Jews, Muslims, and Christians. This has been the promise we have followed through Abraham and Isaac and Jacob: the promise of land to call their own. It became the Promised Land. For the descendants of Abraham, it was *the land* here on this earth that would sustain their lives and ground their identity. Yet all these many years later this land called "home" is still an elusive thing.

Our Father knows we need a home. We need land. We need security. But He tells us that this earth where we roam is only a temporary home. We are wanderers, strangers, pilgrims here. There is a better home, and He is waiting for us—there.

The true home where we are going is lit by the glory of God and watered by the River of Life (Revelation 22:1), and our Father waits for us there. It is impossible to get there on our own. We are too blind and too lost. God has sent His Son to show us the way. He will lead us along a path that isn't paved with good intentions but with repentance and forgiveness.

It's often been said that "I'm sorry" are two of the hardest words for us to say. Here at the end of the story, Joseph's brothers finally came to him and said these hardest words. They couldn't quite bring themselves to say it in their own words, though. They used their father's voice as a posthumous arbitrator to plead for them: "Please forgive your brothers the sins and wrongs they committed in treating you so badly." After all this time, these brothers of Joseph were still filled with dread and fear. The sins they committed against Joseph still haunted them, and they knew they did not deserve forgiveness. And they were right—they didn't.

> And Joseph shows us,
> through his words and actions
> *who* God our Father is:
> "You intended to harm me,
> but God intended it for good
> to accomplish what is now being done;
> the saving of many lives.
> Do not be afraid.
> I will provide for you."
> (Genesis 50:19–21, my paraphrase)

He reassured them. He spoke kindly to them. He loved them. He forgave them. These words are familiar if you know the story of Jesus. He came as Emmanuel, God with us. He came as the good Shepherd to rescue what was lost. He came to show us the way home. He came to do what we could not. He came to give His life as a ransom for many. He came as the perfect Lamb to die a sacrificial Passover death. He came to shed His blood that we may have life. He came to ask for the Father's forgiveness for His brothers and sisters who did not know what they were doing in their sin. And this is the most generous blessing of all: God, our Father, blesses us with life everlasting through forgiveness. It is through this gate of forgiveness that we enter into life. We walk through the gates and are welcomed home.

If you,
like Joseph's brothers,
are still held captive by fear and sorrow
over harm you have caused,
take heart in this story we have read
and lean into it.

Our Father God has come to rescue us. He knows that our sins are many. He knows we cling to death and Satan pursues us. But God, the Creator, created us for life eternal.

Can you turn away from your plans of sin and death? Can you say the hardest words? Can you reach out and take hold of the hand that is offered?

It is stained with blood. There is dirt under the nails.

And it points the way home.

THE END OF THE BEGINNING

Genesis is the beginning of God's relationship with the world. It is the story of a mighty God loving and rescuing the people He created. Was it what you thought it would be?

The people were worse than I had remembered from my childhood days in Sunday school. The violence was more personal and heartless than I would have imagined. The lying and deceit were more calculated and cunning than I expected. I can also relate to those people far more than I care to acknowledge. How could God bear to care for us at all?

These are the things I came to understand about God:

First, above all, God is with us. He was there in the night, showing up with a blazing torch or a stairway to heaven saying, "Here I am. I am with you. I will protect you and give you land—a place to belong. I will give you children—relationships that will span from the past to the present and into the future. You can hide under sheep's clothing, you can try to run away to Egypt, but there is no getting away from Me. Even when you descend into the darkest dungeons and blackest despair, there is one thing that will not change: I am with you."

Another thing about this God: He changes us. Has God been with you as you have read His stories? Has He been wrestling with you—trying to tenderly show you that you need to submit to Him? Or has He shown up to change your name ("You will no longer be known as 'Jane the Cautious,' but now you will be called 'Jane the Confident!'")?

My hope is that God's Word has changed you from the inside out. It may have been dramatic—like Sarah suddenly being pregnant or Jacob limping after a marathon of all-night wrestling. Or it may have been subtle in a day-to-day sort of way—like Joseph slowly maturing within his prison walls or Judah finally realizing he needed to start taking responsibility for his actions.

God tells us His Word is "alive and powerful. It is sharper than the sharpest two-edged sword, cutting between soul and spirit, between joint and marrow. It exposes our innermost thoughts and desires" (Hebrews 4:12 NLT). We have seen Him speak into His world again and again, righting what was horribly wrong and giving life to people who had lost the will to live. This God can change the unchangeable. This God can find a future in the darkest dead end.

In Genesis, we have learned that just as God's words are powerful, *our* words are more important than we may realize. We listened as casual conversations became pivotal: "Why is your face downcast?" or, "I had a dream last night I don't understand." In a moment a nation's destiny changed. God's words are powerful, and He often uses our own words to change our world.

The other thing you couldn't help but notice in these pages of Genesis is that God cares deeply about our relationships:

with Him and with others around us. This larger-than-life Creator God *is smack dab in the middle of relationships.* For the deceiver Jacob, God placed him under his uncle Laban's thumb—a deceiver extraordinaire. Jacob learned that all his manipulations of people and circumstances were pointless—because God alone was in control.

For favorite son Joseph, God placed him as a powerless servant within the powerful household of Potiphar so that he could learn the language, culture, and politics of this foreign land—in preparation for his overnight rise to second in charge of the most powerful nation in the world.

Look around you. What relationships has God placed you in? What is He teaching you? What might He be preparing you for?

> God has been with you
> in His Word,
> in the ever-changing circumstances
>   and conversations of this world,
> and in your relationships,
>   though broken or painful they may be.

God is with you. He created you for great purpose. You are valuable to Him, and He will not let you go quietly into a silent good night without a fight. So tattoo this onto your very soul because you need to know what kind of God you are dealing with:

He is not an unknown "higher power." He is not some vague spirit out there in the universe. He is *your Creator*. Almighty God. He is a God more intentional than you have imagined.

He is more loving than you could have hoped for. And more forgiving than you deserve.

My prayer is that you have discovered a God that you didn't quite believe existed. Draw close to Him. You were made in His image. Take one day at a time, trusting Him along the way. It is going to be a wonderful journey.

FROM THE AUTHOR

It always starts with a story. Mine started in a large family in Greenville, South Carolina. More than my parents and three sisters, it was also an extended family of aunts and uncles and cousins that lived all around us. None were shy, and everyone had a story to tell.

There was a little church just down the road, built on my great-grandfather's land, and that was where I started hearing God's stories.

Farther down the road, in Atlanta, was where I married Jeff, bought a house, then raised a son and a daughter. And I gathered friends and family around my dining table and told stories of my own.

I told the world's stories as a film director for television. I told fictitious stories of Thanksgiving dinners and engagement parties and girls winning the volleyball game. I told true stories of cancer survivors and jewelry designers and girls who were kidnapped and left for dead.

I told God's stories as a teaching director for a Bible study. I told stories of jealous brothers, star-filled nights, and blind men who could suddenly see. I told stories of a Father's love and a Son's devotion and a Spirit that lives inside of those who say yes.

I want you to know these stories. Because it is in our stories that we find God. He is always there. Sometimes, with voice loud, in the middle of the story. Sometimes, quietly waiting on the edge. There is nothing like a good story—especially when God is in the telling.

I blog at smallstoriesofabiggod.com

NOTES

CHAPTER 1

[1] Ray Pritchard, "God in Three Persons: A Doctrine We Barely Understand," Christianity.com, http://www.christianity.com/god/trinity/god-in-three-persons-a-doctrine-we-barely-understand-11634405.html.

CHAPTER 4

[2] Some information in this section on Jude taken from Charles Swindoll, "Jude," Insight for Living Ministries, https://www.insight.org/resources/bible/the-general-epistles/jude.

CHAPTER 5

[3] Some information in this section on the great flood taken from Dr. Monty White, "Flood Legends: The Significance of a World of Stories Based on Truth," Answers in Genesis, https://answersingenesis.org/the-flood/flood-legends/flood-legends/.

[4] "Satellite May Have Found Noah's Ark," ABC NEWS, March 15, 2006, http://abcnews.go.com/GMA/story?id=1727536.

CHAPTER 7

[5] Jody Veenker, "God Speaks to Commuters," *Christianity Today*, July 12, 1999, http://www.christianitytoday.com/ct/1999/july12/9t810c.html.

[6] "History," GodSpeaks, https://godspeaks.com/about/.

CHAPTER 8

[7] "Great Is Thy Faithfulness," Thomas Obediah Chisholm (1866-1960), William Marion Runyan (1870-1957), © 1923. Ren. 1951 Hope Publishing Co., Carol Stream, IL 60188.

CHAPTER 9

[8] "Criticism of the Pledge of Allegiance," Wikipedia, https://en.wikipedia.org/wiki/Criticism_of_the_Pledge_of_Allegiance.

[9] "Allegiance," Merriam-Webster, https://www.merriam-webster.com/dictionary/allegiance.

[10] "Ally," Merriam-Webster, https://www.merriam-webster.com/dictionary/ally.

[11] Galyn Wiemers, "Salem, Jebus or Jerusalem," Jerusalem 101, http://www.generationword.com/jerusalem101/16-salem-jebus.html.

CHAPTER 10

[12] "A Canyon Alight With Stars: A Brief History of Astronomy at Bryce Canyon National Park," National Park Service: Bryce Canyon, https://www.nps.gov/brca/planyourvisit/astrohistory.htm.

[13] Note on Genesis 15:5, NIV Study Bible, Google Books, https://books.google.com/books?id=VVOzRVQcD3sC&printsec=frontcover&dq=isbn:0310437423&hl=en&sa=X&ved=0ahUKEwi685rG_-rVAhVI7CYKHXVEC18Q6AEIKDAA#v=onepage&q=stars&f=false.

[14] Seth M. Rodriquez, "The Land of Israel ... Why There?," Wild Olive Shoot, http://wild-olive-shoot.blogspot.com/2012/01/land-of-israel-why-there.html.

CHAPTER 12

[15] Cory Baugher, "The Meaning of El Shaddai," Knowing the Bible, https://www.knowingthebible.net/the-meaning-of-el-shaddai.

CHAPTER 15

[16] See Luke 4:18–19 and Isaiah 61:1–2.

[17] See Luke 10:11.

[18] See Matthew 16:27.

[19] Carolyn A. Roth, "Abraham Planted Tamarisk Trees," God as a Gardener, https://godasagardener.com/2011/03/24/abraham-the-tamarisk/.

CHAPTER 17

[20] See Genesis 12:1.

[21] James Orr, "Hebron (2)," Bible Study Tools, http://www.biblestudytools.com/dictionary/hebron/.

[22] "Hebron: City, West Bank," Encyclopædia Britannica, https://www.britannica.com/place/Hebron-city-West-Bank.

CHAPTER 18

[23] "Do the Humps on Camels Hold Water?," HowStuffWorks.com, http://animals.howstuffworks.com/mammals/question104.htm.

[24] Anne Helmenstine, "How Much Does a Gallon of Water Weigh? Easy Calculation," ScienceNotes.org, https://sciencenotes.org/much-gallon-water-weigh-easy-calculation/.

CHAPTER 19

[25] "What Is the Significance of 'Firstborn' in the Bible?," Bible.org, https://bible.org/question/what-significance-"firstborn"-bible.

CHAPTER 22

[26] Robert Frost, "Mending Wall," in The Poetry of Robert Frost, ed. Edward Connery Lathem (New York: Holt, Rinehart and Winston, 1969), 33–34.

CHAPTER 23

[27] "Etymology of the Name Jacob," Abarim Publications, http://www.abarim-publications.com/Meaning/Jacob.html#.Waf8stQrKHs.

CHAPTER 25

[28] Walter L. Baker, "Obadiah," The Bible Knowledge Commentary: An Exposition of the Scriptures (Old Testament), eds. John F. Walvoord and Roy B. Zuck (Colorado Springs, CO: David C Cook, 1985), 1454–1455.

[29] Henry H. Halley, Halley's Bible Handbook (Grand Rapids, MI: Zondervan, 1962), 284.

CHAPTER 27

[30] Rick Warren, The Purpose Driven Life: What on Earth Am I Here for? (Grand Rapids, MI: Zondervan, 2002), 173.

[31] Warren W. Wiersbe, The Bumps Are What You Climb On: Encouragement for Difficult Days (Grand Rapids, MI: Baker), 114.

CHAPTER 29

[32] "Sovereign," YourDictionary.com, http://law.yourdictionary.com/sovereign.

[33] "We Don't See Things as They Are, We See Them as We Are," Quote Investigator, https://quoteinvestigator.com/2014/03/09/as-we-are/#note-8403-3.

[34] Doug McIntosh, "Parallels between the Life of Joseph and Jesus Christ," Genesis: Volume 2 (Colorado Springs, CO: Community Bible Study, 2008), 154–155.

CHAPTER 30

[35] I apologize for my lack of a specific source here, but a great deal of online research showed that the authorship and copyright of this song are still under debate. It seems that it may be an old folk song that carried forward through the years until it was sung in modern times by artists such as Johnny Cash, whose version I am familiar with. With that in mind, I'll refer you to those lyrics: "I Am A Pilgrim," AZLyrics.com, https://www.azlyrics.com/lyrics/johnnycash/iamapilgrim.html.

CHAPTER 32

[36] "Hebron: Tomb of the Patriarchs (Ma'arat HaMachpelah)," Jewish Virtual Library, http://www.jewishvirtuallibrary.org/tomb-of-the-patriarchs-ma-arat-hamachpelah.